AIR UNIVERSITY

CARL A. SPAATZ CENTER FOR OFFICER EDUCATION

AIR FORCE FELLOWS

Rethinking the QDR
The Case for a Persistent Defense Review

P. Dean Patterson, Jr.
Lieutenant Colonel, USMC

Lenny J. Richoux
Lieutenant Colonel, USAF

Walker Paper No. 14

Air University Press
Maxwell Air Force Base, Alabama 36112-5962

January 2009

Muir S. Fairchild Research Information Center Cataloging Data

Patterson, P. Dean.
    Rethinking the QDR : the case for a persistent defense review / P. Dean Patterson,
Jr., Lenny J. Richoux.
        p. ; cm. – (Walker paper, 1555-7871 ; no. 14)
    Includes bibliographical references.

    1. Military planning—United States. 2. National security—United States. 3. Spe-
cial operations (Military science)—United States—Forecasting. 4. United States—
Military Policy. I. Richoux, Lenny J. II. Title. III. Series: Walker paper (Maxwell Air
Force Base, Ala.) ; no. 14.

    355.033/73—dc22

Disclaimer

This Walker Paper and others in the series are available
electronically at the Air University Research Web site
http://research.maxwell.af.mil and the AU Press Web
site http://aupress.maxwell.af.mil.

Air Force Fellows

Since 1958, the Air Force has assigned a small number of carefully chosen, experienced officers to serve one-year tours at distinguished civilian institutions studying national security policy and strategy. Beginning with the 1994 academic year, these programs were accorded senior service school professional military education in-residence credit. In 2003 these fellowships assumed senior developmental education (SDE), force development credit for eligible officers.

The SDE-level Air Force Fellows serve as visiting military ambassadors to their centers, devoting effort to expanding their colleagues' understanding of defense matters. As such, candidates for SDE-level fellowships have a broad knowledge of key Department of Defense (DOD) and Air Force issues. SDE-level fellows perform outreach by their presence and voice in sponsoring institutions. They are expected to provide advice as well as promote and explain Air Force and DOD policies, programs, and military-doctrine strategy to nationally recognized scholars, foreign dignitaries, and leading policy analysts. The Air Force Fellows also gain valuable perspectives from the exchange of ideas with these civilian leaders. SDE-level fellows are expected to apprise appropriate Air Force agencies of significant developments and emerging views on defense as well as economic and foreign policy issues within their centers. Each fellow is expected to use the unique access she or he has as grounds for research and writing on important national security issues. The SDE Air Force Fellows include the National Defense Fellows, the RAND Fellows, the National Security Fellows, and the Secretary of Defense Corporate Fellows. The Air Force Fellows also support a post-SDE military fellow at the Council on Foreign Relations.

On the level of intermediate developmental education, the chief of staff approved several Air Force Fellowships focused on career broadening for Air Force majors. The Air Force Legislative Fellows was established in April 1995, with the Foreign Policy Fellowship and Defense Advanced Research Projects Agency Fellowship coming under the Air Force Fellows program in 2003. In 2004 the AF Fellows also assumed responsibility of the National Laboratories Technologies Fellows.

Contents

CONTENTS

Illustrations

Figure

Foreword

Consider the millions of man-hours spent by talented, highly educated military officers, the number of contractors who are anxiously awaiting a chance to get in the fight, or the political appointees who are nervously awaiting the next step. Sound like someone planning a war? In a way, it is. Legislation mandating a DOD quadrennial defense review (QDR) was passed in 1997, yielding three detailed, thoughtful reports about the next vector our armed services should take. The services took on a war-like posture as each one approached. The next QDR, due to the Congress nine months after the next presidential inauguration, promises another such pitched battle. A look back at service budgets that resulted after past QDRs tells the story. Each service maintains its fair share of the DOD budget. If we already know the answer, why the fuss? Aside from the fact that it's the law, there is too much national treasure at stake not to take a harder look every four years. The DOD's base budget for fiscal year (FY) 07 is $432 billion and $481 billion for FY 08. To ensure that the DOD is properly managing taxpayer's money while still providing the best for our soldiers, sailors, Airmen, and marines, we must not pay just lip service to this upcoming QDR.

The QDR serves as a strategic pause, a chance to get inside the Pentagon's cycle of planning, programming, budgeting, and executing—a systems analysis approach to defense planning created by Robert McNamara. It provides a unique opportunity for Congress to evaluate past investments as they relate to ongoing and future demands. In that sense, it is good. It also provides the necessary cross-checks on the DOD budget, which accounts for 4.3 percent of the US gross domestic product and, in 2005, 41 percent of all world military outlays. Past QDRs have been characterized as down-top, or leadership-driven, or bottom-up, starting from nothing and building a notionally "correct" future military force. At a time when we are faced with unknown potential national security crises, we should begin now to shape a relatively new and maturing QDR: scrap it, modify it, or enlarge it. Some say the QDR should go away altogether. But, a more pragmatic alternative would be to shape the existing legislation. With the upcoming elections guaranteeing a new administration, extending the QDR's deadline beyond 30 September 2009 will allow a new president more time to evaluate the merits of a report started by the current administration.

Because changing the legislation may prove difficult, DOD could consider internal changes. Instead of ramping up the services for a QDR every four years, why not have a persistent QDR? The intellect, manpower, and data are always resident. This approach requires a disciplined, persistent, and honest look at least quarterly, and it could narrow the gap between those who determine requirements, manage defense programs, and execute budgets. The Pentagon is notoriously good at planning. Often, it is more difficult to translate those plans into budgets and hardware; therein lies the challenge. An even bolder proposition would be to enlarge the QDR, transforming it from a defense review to a national security review. The apparent interagency cooperation dilemmas remain, but the process could spark the wider improvements that the Goldwater-Nichols Act of 1986 brought to DOD. This alternative would clearly open the defense budget to the rest of the national security establishment, for better or worse.

The next QDR likely will examine a portfolio of difficult challenges. Among these are the ongoing conflicts in Afghanistan and Iraq, development of a more robust counter-insurgency capability, the threats of nuclear-capable North Korea and Iran, and the rise of such near-peer competitors as China. There is a window of opportunity to mature the QDR in very good ways. It should be about collaboration, not compromise. The next QDR should focus on a short list of strategic initiatives agreed upon by the secretary and chairman, with buy-in from the service chiefs. Further, the QDR should encompass dialogue, not discussion. The services are the experts at their military crafts and symbiotically contribute to our overall national defense. In that tone, the QDR should not be a pitched battle over programs and budget or zero-sum game. The QDR is a fairly new DOD process and imperfect, but it is a good reflection of democracy at work, giving voice to every branch of the armed services. It provides the Congress with a view of taxpayer money outside of the context of congressional markups. Like Democracy, it is slow, hard, and frustrating but the alternative is unsatisfactory and potentially disastrous.

Lenny J. Richoux
Lieutenant Colonel, USAF

About the Authors

Lt Col P. Dean Patterson, Jr.

Lt Col Dean Patterson, US Marine Corps, is an aviation command and control officer, Aviation Command and Control Branch, Department of Aviation, Headquarters US Marine Corps. Colonel Patterson, a former Air Force enlisted Airman, was commissioned in the US Marine Corps in 1988 through the officer candidate school located at Quantico, Virginia.

After completing the air support officer course, he was assigned to the Marine Corps Air Support Squadron-3, 3d Marine Aviation Wing, Camp Pendleton, California, as an air support control officer. Since 1988 he has had various assignments, including instructor and company executive officer, Marine Corps Communication-Electronic School, 29 Palms, California; operations officer, Marine Air Support Squadron, Camp Pendleton, California; assistant plans officer, Marine Air Control Group-38, Quantico, Virginia; aide-de-camp to the deputy commandant, Manpower and Reserve Affairs, and plans officer, Marine Air Control Group-38, Miramar, California. He also served as the commandant of the Marine Corps Fellows, the Center for a New American Security in Washington, DC.

In support of Operations Desert Shield and Desert Storm, Colonel Patterson deployed with the 2d Marine Division as part of the division's air support element. As the officer in charge of MTACS-38, he supported combat operations as part of Operation Iraqi Freedom II.

Colonel Patterson received his bachelor of science degree in biology from Cumberland College, Williamsburg, Virginia, and his master's degree in education from Chapman University in Orange, California. He is a resident graduate of the Marine Corps Amphibious Warfare School, the Weapons and Tactics Instructor Course, and a nonresident graduate of the Marine Corps Command and Staff program.

Col Lenny J. Richoux

Lt Col Lenny J. Richoux is chief of the Integrated Plans and Strategy Division for the director of communications, secretary of the Air Force, the Pentagon, Washington, DC. He received his bachelor of science degree in aerospace engineering from Georgia Institute of Technology and was commissioned as a second lieutenant in the Air Force through the Air Force Reserve Officer Training Corps program in 1989. After completing pilot training at Columbus Air Force Base (AFB), Mississippi, he reported to Loring AFB, Maine, where he served as a KC-135R pilot with the 42d Air Refueling Squadron. Following his Loring AFB assignment, Colonel Richoux completed many other assignments, including service on the Air Staff as a member of the first Air Force Intern Program, Washington, DC; long-range strategic planner, deputy chief of staff, plans and programs, Headquarters US Air Force; and war planner, operations directorate, J-3, on the Joint Staff.

He commanded the 17th Airlift Squadron at Charleston AFB, South Carolina, and the 816th Expeditionary Airlift Squadron at Al Udeid Air Base, Qatar, before his selection as a National Defense Fellow at the Center for New American Security in Washington, DC. He is a command pilot with more than 3,000 hours in T-37B, T-38A, KC-135A/R/T, and C-17A aircraft.

Colonel Richoux is a graduate of the Air Command and Staff College, Maxwell AFB, Alabama, and holds a master's degree in organizational development and management from George

Washington University. His personal awards include the Defense Meritorious Service Medal, the Meritorious Service Medal with three oak leaf clusters, and the Air Medal with one oak leaf cluster. Effective 1 October 2008, Lieutenant Colonel Richoux achieved the rank of colonel.

Abstract

The fourth Department of Defense (DOD) Quadrennial Defense Review (QDR) will be submitted to Congress in February 2009. A relatively new instrument, the QDR requires the US military establishment to re-examine long-range strategy and adjust the strategic, programmatic, and budgetary vectors of the department. The espoused purpose of the QDR is to survey future national security threats and develop dissuasive strategies. Because strategies eventually lead to programs and budgets, some say that changes to the defense budget are the most important and visible outcomes of the QDR. While the Pentagon's planning, programming, budgeting, and execution (PPBE) system has continuously operated (in one form or another) since the 1960s, the QDR is a relatively recent innovation—with the first report completed in 1997. Since 1997 it has been used by new presidents to mold DOD initiatives and direction at the outset of their administrations. Making such presidential input stick over a four-year term, however, remains a political challenge. While the ongoing PPBE process has served DOD well, the record for the QDR is less solid. Having interviewed several experts with extensive high-level QDR experience, the authors found three popular recommendations on the future of QDR: abandon the QDR; enlarge the QDR to include the interagency; or create a persistent QDR that works alongside the existing PPBE process. An interagency QDR expansion is introduced as an important option but one that will need a longer time horizon to fully implement. This paper examines past QDRs and recommends that DOD adopt a persistent QDR.

Preface and Acknowledgments

Every four years the Department of Defense (DOD) conducts a congressionally mandated strategy review, called the Quadrennial Defense Review (QDR). This process consumes much time, labor, and energy across the DOD. On the positive side, proponents of the QDR claim that strategy changes generated by previous QDRs have led to changes in service personnel levels and equipment purchases that eventually resulted in appropriate shifts in the defense budget. Opponents of the QDR charge that it yields no real change and that it does not contribute to the debate on the future of US defense strategy, policy, programs, and budgets. The answer lies somewhere in the middle—the QDR is necessary, but it can be improved.

This study highlights strengths and weaknesses of the process and provides recommendations for improvement. As such, it should prove useful for future DOD policy makers desiring to improve the QDR and service staffs wishing to gain process insights. In writing this paper, the authors conducted a series of authoritative interviews with individuals who worked on past QDRs. In particular, the authors would like to thank Adm Dennis Blair (USN, retired), Thomas Hafer (US Marine Corps), Jim Thomas (Applied Minds, Inc.), Mark Gunzinger (Office of the Secretary of Defense, Force Transformation), Lisa Disbrow (Office of the Joint Chiefs of Staff J-8), and Kathleen Hicks (Center for Strategic and International Studies). We would also like to thank Michele Flournoy, president and co-founder of the Center for a New American Security and one of the foremost QDR authorities and primary contributor to the 1997 QDR. Her firsthand knowledge and guidance were indispensible. Lastly, but most importantly, we would like to thank Dr. Jim Miller, director of studies, the Center for a New American Security, for guiding, encouraging, and supporting us. The authors are grateful for the support of their services—the US Air Force and US Marine Corps—and specifically Col Mike Davis, Air University, and Mike Cooper and Andrea Hamlen, Marine Corps University, who provided detailed line editing and insightful recommendations. From a broader perspective, this report informs the next and future administrations on how to better manage the Pentagon.

Chapter 1

Introduction

Government is not reason, it is not eloquence, it is force;
like fire, a troublesome servant and a fearful master.
Never for a moment should it be left to irresponsible
action.

—George Washington

Legislation mandating a Department of Defense (DOD) quadrennial defense review (QDR) was passed in 1997. Since 1997
the DOD has developed three detailed, thoughtful reports about
the direction our armed services should take. The next QDR,
due to Congress in 2010 along with the next president's first
budget, is already under way—months before the 2008 presidential election. A look back at service budgets that resulted
after past QDRs tells the story: each service ends up maintain-
ing its fair share (percentage) of the defense budget. The recent
fiscal year (FY) 2009 presidential budget shows the services'
apportionment basically detailed as follows: the Army receiving
a 27 percent share; Air Force, 28 percent share; and, Navy, to
include the Marine Corps, 29 percent. If we already know the
answer, then why all the fuss? Aside from the fact that it's the
law, there is too much national treasure at stake not to conduct
a thorough defense review. DOD's base budget is $515.4 billion
for FY 09. This does not include funds marked for Operations
Enduring Freedom and Iraqi Freedom. To ensure defense is
properly managing taxpayers' money, while still providing the
best for our soldiers, sailors, Airmen, and marines, the QDR
must continue to get the hard look it deserves and has received.

The QDR serves as a strategic pause,[1] a chance to look inside
the Pentagon's cycle of planning, programming, budgeting, and
executing—a systems analysis approach to defense planning
created by Robert S. McNamara. It provides a unique opportunity for Congress to evaluate past investments as they relate to
ongoing and future demands. The QDR also provides the necessary cross-checks on the DOD budget that account for 4.3

1

percent of the US gross domestic product (GDP) and, in 2005, 43 percent of the world's military outlays.[2]

Past defense reviews have been generally characterized as top-down, leadership-driven, or bottom-up, starting from nothing and building a notionally correct future military force. The QDR was shaped by the Commission on Roles and Missions, called the Bottom-Up Review in the early 1990s. In fact, three QDRs have concluded since the 1990s—in 1996, 2001, and 2006. While there is likely not enough time to change the processes governing the QDR for 2009, defense reviewers must begin immediately to take a long view on potential options for shaping a relatively new and maturing QDR: scrap it completely, enlarge it in scope, or stretch it.

Given the perspective of successes and failures of past defense reviews, this study recommends changes for future QDR processes. Some reviewers believe the QDR should go away completely. Other reviewers contend that service rivalries yield static defense budget shares and ultimately break down cooperation and jointness. Further, with so much talent and manpower already at work in the Pentagon, why stand up a separate defense analysis on top of those already in place? Still, scrapping the QDR altogether is probably not the best medicine—a point to be expanded later in the paper.

Still others believe the larger national security apparatus should enlarge the QDR, thus transforming it from a defense review to a national security review. They also want to adapt the idea of a defense review to include, for example, intelligence, homeland security, and state. The apparent interagency cooperation dilemmas remain, but the process could spark the wider improvements that the Goldwater-Nichols Act of 1986 brought to the Defense Department. This alternative clearly opens the defense budget to the rest of the national security establishment, for better or worse. The enlargement option will be discussed briefly, but it is not the primary recommendation for the *immediate* future of the QDR. An interagency review would be tremendously useful; this paper recommends changes that can be implemented without depending upon change to public law pertaining to the QDR.

Yet another option is to broaden the QDR so that the Defense Department takes a persistent look at the process, like the current PPBE system, instead of once every four years, and expands it into a persistent QDR (PQDR). This approach requires a disciplined, persistent, and honest look perhaps on a quarterly basis. In addition, it could narrow the gap between those who determine requirements, manage defense programs, and execute budgets. The Pentagon is notoriously good at operational planning but is challenged by the task of translating strategies into acquisition programs and budgets. Still, with proper checks, the existing staff could provide the requisite information for real-time defense reviews.

The best solution is probably a combination of the latter two of these alternatives and would result in a persistent, enlarged QDR, phased-in throughout every level of government, from Congress down to the services. Scrapping elements of the QDR proven ineffective might also be considered. This paper endorses the PQDR concept as the one with the greatest promise for near-term positive change that can be implemented within DOD.

The next QDR likely will examine several difficult challenges. These include the ongoing conflicts in Afghanistan and Iraq, development of a more robust counter-insurgency capability, the threats of nuclear-capable North Korea and Iran, and the rise of near-peer competitors, such as China. A window of opportunity allows the QDR to mature in many ways. First, the QDR should emphasize collaboration, not compromise. Second, the next QDR should focus on a short list of strategic initiatives, agreed upon by the secretary and chairman, with buy-in from the service chiefs. Third, the QDR should embrace dialogue. Traditionally, the services present a strategy with accompanying budget requirements and typically do not deviate from this position as the QDR progresses. The QDR should not display a pitched battle over programs and budget in a zero-sum game atmosphere. Instead, the services should contribute their individual strengths symbiotically to the overall national defense. The paper also examines how the Marine Corps and Air Force may approach the current and future QDRs (appendix E).

Notes

(All notes appear in shortened form. For full details, see the appropriate entry in the bibliography.)

1. Thomas Hafer, interview by authors, 1 November 2007.
2. Benton, CIS (Computer Information System) 350–Computers, Society, and Ethics.

Chapter 2

Background

The Secretary of Defense shall every four years . . . conduct a comprehensive examination (to be known as a "quadrennial defense review") of the national defense strategy, force structure, force modernization plans, infrastructure, budget plan, and other elements of the defense program and policies of the United States with a view toward determining and expressing the defense strategy of the United States and establishing a defense program for the next 20 years.

—*Congressional Record*, 5 August 1999, H7527

The Goldwater-Nichols Reorganization Act of 1986 was the most far reaching of defense reorganizations since the National Security Act of 1947. In 1986 the Packard Commission made far-reaching recommendations to reorganize the Defense Department. In response, the DOD initiated the 1989 defense management review, which outlined ways to improve acquisition strategies and oversight during the George H. W. Bush presidential administration. This study resulted in the 1991 base force that was framed by then-Joint Chiefs of Staff (JCS) chairman, Gen Colin Powell, and Defense Secretary Dick Cheney. At the beginning of the Bill Clinton administration, Defense Secretary Les Aspin produced the October 1993 Bottom-Up Review—a study intended to address post–Cold War restructuring requirements. A commission on roles and missions was required by the FY 94 Defense Authorization Act to evaluate the military's structure. The commission suggested a need to conduct a four-year review of DOD strategy, which resulted in the creation of the QDR. The QDR is a wide-ranging review of all elements of defense policy and strategy needed to support national security strategy and involves the Office of the Secretary of Defense (OSD), JCS, the combatant commanders, and the services. Congress then formulates law enacting or modifies the recommendations of the QDR. The defense secretary and the chairman of the JCS oversee the QDR process.[1]

The legislation mandating the QDR is the National Defense Authorization Act of 1996, Public Law 104-201 (appendices A and B). In response to the recommendations of the Commission on Roles and Missions of the Armed Forces, the secretary of defense endorsed the concept of conducting a quadrennial review of its defense program at the beginning of each newly elected presidential administration. The first review was planned to involve a comprehensive examination of defense strategy; force structure of the active, guard, and reserve components; force modernization, infrastructure; and elements of the defense program and policies "to determine and express the defense strategy of the United States and to establish a revised defense program through the year 2005."[2]

1997 QDR

The QDR of 1997 reaffirmed the force-sizing construct of fighting and winning two overlapping major theater wars. At that time, the DOD recommended that the United States needed to retain this commitment to avoid losing the confidence of its allies and to be prepared to respond to a full range of threats.[3] There was also an emphasis on preparing for future smaller-scale contingencies, entailing limited intensities and objectives.[4] At the same time that the DOD prepared for the QDR, it prepared *Joint Vision (JV) 2010*[5]—the latter as the chairman's vision for a revolution in military affairs. JV 2010 espoused that the US military should be prepared to conduct the full range of military operations from humanitarian assistance and peace operations to full-scale war.[6] The secretary of defense also believed that the services needed to address the aging force problem. Another objective of the QDR of 1996 was to increase the DOD's procurement budget (with a target of $60 billion) to achieve its modernization agenda.

The QDR of 1997 was considered both a bottom-up and top-down examination. It was bottom-up because it utilized expertise from throughout the DOD, but it also solicited ideas outside the department. It was considered top-down because the secretary of defense and chairman guided the process. However, the secretary of defense did not have as much ownership as did his predecessor.

The QDR of 1997 was structured at three organizational levels. First, seven panels conducted reviews of strategy, force structure, readiness, modernization, infrastructure, human resources, information operations, and intelligence. At the second level, an integration group organized the panel results into a set of options—each designed for consistency with defense strategy. At the third level, a senior steering group, co-chaired by the deputy secretary of defense and the vice chairman, JCS, oversaw the entire process and made recommendations to the defense secretary. Additionally, the National Defense Panel received regular briefings on the work of the panels and on the integration options and decisions. The National Security Council staff and other administration agencies also participated at various points in the review. As decision options began to take shape, the DOD began to consult with Congress.[7]

National Defense Panel Summary

The 1996 defense authorization bill included the Lieberman Amendment, which established a national defense panel to "review, assess, and provide Congress with an alternative view to that provided by the Pentagon." The panel, appointed by the defense secretary in consultation with Congress, was to include independent, nonpartisan, private-sector military experts. However, the panel was often criticized for containing too many defense establishment insiders to be truly independent.

The National Defense Panel report of December 1997 identified several initiatives to meet perceived future challenges. Specifically, it recommended that the United States undertake a broad transformation of its national security structures, operational concepts and equipment, and DOD business processes. Finally, bringing together all the elements of America's national power would demand a highly integrated and responsive national security community to actively plan for the future—one that molds the international environment rather than merely responds to it. This report encourages the DOD to continue building on the Goldwater–Nichols reforms and to extend a sense of jointness beyond the department to the rest of the national security establishment and to our friends and allies abroad.[8]

2001 QDR

In 2001 Secretary of Defense Donald Rumsfeld employed the QDR to outline his vision of transforming how DOD would conduct operations. His basic proposition, as he indicated in his preface to the QDR, was that "a new strategy for America's defense . . . would embrace uncertainty and contend with surprise, a strategy premised on the idea that to be effective abroad, America must be safe at home."[9]

The resultant QDR strategy was built around four key goals to guide the development, capabilities, deployment, and use of US forces: "assuring allies and friends of the United States' steadiness of purpose and its capability to fulfill its security commitments; dissuading adversaries from undertaking programs or operations that could threaten U.S. interests or those of our allies and friends; deterring aggression and coercion by deploying forward the capacity to swiftly defeat attacks and impose severe penalties for aggression on an adversary's military capability and supporting infrastructure; and, decisively defeating any adversary if deterrence fails."[10]

The QDR of 2001 also introduced capabilities-based planning. This concept focused on how an adversary might fight rather than specifically who the adversary might be or where a war might occur. This concept recognized that it was not enough to plan for large conventional wars in distant theaters. Instead, the DOD was to identify the capabilities required to deter and defeat adversaries who will rely on surprise, deception, and asymmetric warfare to achieve their objectives.[11]

Pentagon officials say there was some thought given after the 9/11 attacks to putting off the QDR report, which was due to Congress on 30 September, to review in depth how the events of 9/11 should affect military planning. But defense leaders decided instead to proceed on the notion that the QDR already included attention to homeland defense, asymmetric threats, and potential surprises and that references to the terrorist attacks could be added to the existing document.[12] Even though the secretary of defense saw the QDR as an opportunity to transform the DOD, a majority of his time and effort was rightly spent with the United States engaged in combat operations in Afghanistan and Iraq.

The 2001 QDR process was considered top-down because decisions were made among the most-senior DOD leadership. The terms of reference in its unclassified form comprised 22 pages and basically said "U. S. forces overall remain unrivaled, but are largely a downsized legacy of Cold War investment and therefore may not be optimized for the future." Also, central to the review was a shift in defense planning from a threat-based model that had dominated thinking in the past to a capabilities-based model for the future.[13]

The QDR of 2001 was structured at several organizational levels. The first level comprised eight integrated project teams (IPT) that conducted reviews of strategy and force planning; military organizations and arrangements; capabilities and systems; space, information, and intelligence; forces, personnel, and readiness; and infrastructure and integration. At the second level, an executive working group (EWG) was created and charged with promulgating the secretary of defense's guidance and with overseeing a mechanism for integrating analysis, products, and deliverables for decisions by the secretary of defense.[14] Finally, a senior-level review group was established as the decision-making body. The group, led by the secretary of defense and the deputy secretary of defense, included the JCS chairman, the service secretaries, and the undersecretaries of defense.

2006 QDR

The QDR of 2006 was submitted in the fifth year of America's global war on terror, or long war. The QDR of 2006 was to help shape the process of change within the DOD and to provide the United States with strong, sound, and effective war-fighting capabilities. Deputy secretary of defense Gordon England's assessment of the QDR of 2006 portrayed this effort as the first contemporary defense review to coincide with an ongoing major conflict. This compelled the DOD to recast its view of future warfare through the lens of a long-duration conflict and in the midst of two stabilization campaigns.

This review required a judicious balance between present needs and future capabilities. The aim was a review that was strategy driven, capabilities focused, and budget disciplined. The department enjoyed additional time to organize, deliberate on, and craft the review because of an extended submission suspense granted by Congress.[15]

The QDR of 2006 continued a shift that began with the QDR of 2001 away from the planning construct of the 1990s that had focused on a requirement to fight "two major theater wars." Drawing on an assumption that the day-to-day or steady-state operational tempo for US forces would continue to be high even without Iraq and Afghanistan, the QDR of 2006 refined a force-planning construct to include the steady-state and surge requirements for three objective areas: homeland defense, war on terror/irregular warfare, and conventional campaigns.[16]

Some programming decisions were made during the QDR of 2006, including the plus up of special operating forces (SOF), the increase in civil affairs and psychological operations, and the commitment to a next-generation, long-range bomber and new tanker fleet. Although not driven by the QDR, the Air Force cut its personnel levels by 40,000 in hopes of a successful cost trade-off to allow recapitalization and systems' modernization. At nearly the same time of the post-2006 QDR, the Army and Marine Corps increased end-strengths due to operational commitments.

To summarize an assessment by Andy Krepinevich at the Center for Strategic and Budgetary Analysis, the QDR got the challenges right, did okay on strategy, but failed to make tough choices for budget and programming. The result, he says, means the DOD will invest "increasingly scarce resources in capabilities optimized for the 'wrong future.'"[17] The authors assert, however, that the QDR of 2006 successfully bridged strategy to budget, with a direct impact on the office of the secretary of defense's bottom line and division of resources.

Many believe the secretary of defense was as deeply involved in the development of the QDR of 2006 as he was in 2001. Although the department called the QDR of 2006 "leadership-driven," the secretary of defense handed off day-to-day responsibility to the undersecretary of defense for policy.[18]

The various QDR 2006 IPTs were highly integrated bodies, with representatives of the services, combatant commands, OSD, interagency and even international partners. Indeed, when compared to other defense reviews, the QDR of 2006 was notably more transparent and inclusive.[19] Each study team had senior civilian and military leadership, and the team leaders worked together to share findings and avoid duplication and other deficiencies.[20] This all required a massive commitment of resources, with hundreds of DOD and non-DOD personnel involved in the various groups. Despite all this transparency, the DOD chose not to conduct regular consultations with senior congressional leadership, leading the House Armed Services Committee to conduct its own committee defense review.

Although the secretary's senior leadership review group was the senior organization, in practice, the deputy's advisory working group (DAWG)—led by the deputy secretary and vice chairman of the Joint Chiefs of Staff and included the service vice chiefs, the undersecretaries of defense, and other key officials—became the final arbiter of recommendations from each IPT. The director of program analysis and evaluation managed the process, guiding the recommendations of each study team through a gauntlet of reviews on their way to what came to be affectionately known as the "DAWG."

General Observations

The QDR is a relatively young and still-evolving process. Examining the previous defense reviews, a few evolutionary trends come to light. One common thread is level of interest. Because service budgets are at stake, no player wishes to leave his or her seat vacant at the QDR table. The result has been a process with too many players, adding ambiguity and clouding the difficult strategy decisions that could drive budget. Because the QDR is conducted infrequently, participant expectations are perhaps unreasonably high. This could lead to the failure to achieve actionable goals.

Regarding how presidential administrations have handled the QDR, one apparent difference lies in whether it was conducted under a first- or second-term administration. First-term administrations seem to favor a more closed process and have

11

higher expectations of major changes, whereas second-term administrations appear to have a more open process and have a more realistic expectation level. A new administration also seems to possess the greatest opportunity for change but, depending upon the political climate, may be the least capable of realizing those changes.[21] In addition, current military operations or national security threats tend to influence the QDR's direction. Such significant events as the end of the Cold War, Somalia, and 9/11 look to have been the biggest catalysts for change. Short of major world events, big changes in defense programs appear to require considerable time and effort.

Notes

1. Brower, "QDR for Dummies."
2. National Defense Authorization Act of 1996, 921–26.
3. DOD News Briefing "Quadrennial Defense Review."
4. Tangredi, "All Possible Wars?"
5. DOD News Briefing, "Quadrennial Defense Review."
6. Peters, "Joint Vision 2010 Still Focusing."
7. DOD, QDR of 1997, section 1.
8. Blaker, "QDR." The nine panel members included Robert RisCassi, a retired Army general who was a Lockheed Martin vice president; a retired Marine general who was a managing director of McDonnell Douglas-Europe; a retired Navy admiral and former chairman, JCS, who was the CEO of Technology Strategies and Alliances; and Janne Nolan, a senior fellow at the Brookings Institute. The panel chairman was Phil Odeen, head of BDM International, an IT company.
9. DOD, "Quadrennial Defense Review of 2001," iii.
10. Ibid., iii–iv.
11. Ibid.
12. Grossman, "Key Review Offers Scant Guidance on Handling '4th Generation' Threats," 1.
13. Correll, "In Pursuit of a Strategy."
14. Guidance and Terms of Reference for the 2001 Quadrennial Defense Review.
15. DOD, "Chairman's Assessment of the 2006 Quadrennial Defense Review."
16. Ibid., 16–18.
17. Krepinevich, "Quadrennial Defense Review," 14.
18. Government Accounting Office (GAO), "Quadrennial Defense Review," 10.
19. Ibid.
20. Ibid., 14.
21. Flournoy, remarks, "Goldwater-Nichols."

Chapter 3

Alternatives for the Next QDR

Doctor: "How does it hurt?"
Patient: "It only hurts when I breathe."
"Doctor: "So, stop doing that."

—Unknown

With a historical perspective on the evolution of the QDR, this study lays out three alternatives for future reviews and recommends a persistent approach for future reviews. Although the QDR was created by Congress, the current body of legislators appears not to know what to do with the document—possibly resulting from repetitive briefings on future capabilities and stagnant budget allocations between the services.[1] This chapter examines the possibilities of doing away with the QDR, enlarging the QDR to include the entire national security apparatus, or creating a persistent QDR (PQDR). While all three will be introduced and briefly discussed, moving toward a PQDR is recommended and will be unpacked.

Many critics of the QDR believe it has outlived its usefulness and should be discontinued. Tom Donnelly's "Kill the QDR" states that "After four attempts (if you include the 1993 Bottom-Up Review), it is fair to conclude that the process has outlived its utility."[2] In sum, beginning in 1993, the Quadrennial Defense Review process has fallen short of what it was intended to do: provide a persistent link among strategy, force planning, and defense budgeting. Indeed, with every QDR, the situation has grown worse; the ends-means problem has grown. In other words, as US national security responsibilities grow, it is becoming increasingly difficult to develop strategy that is prioritized and constrained within a finite defense budget.

Doing away with the QDR requires a change in legislation; these changes could be implemented within the current legislative framework. Another option would be to enlarge the QDR to include the broader interagency involved in national security: a quadrennial national security review (QNSR). This option is more challenging to implement but could open previously muted lines of communication and blend functional interagency stove-pipes. Yet another option would be a persistent QDR. The authors' definition of a PDQR is a defense review that is continuous but reports quarterly. It recognizes the existing battle rhythm within the Pentagon and would capitalize upon existing staffs, studies, processes, and organizations to make the QDR a more dynamic instrument that adapts and is responsive to changes in the defense environment. It should blend with the existing PPBE process to ensure presidential priorities remain alive, relevant, and acted upon. The effect of a properly implemented PQDR allows the DOD to answer QDR-related questions every day vice just once every four years. An introduction of each option follows.

Cancel the QDR

QDRs often inspire hope at the outset and disappointment upon conclusion; they seldom seem to live up to their potential. Given the budgetary and strategy challenges, the nation needs QDRs to break that mold.[2] Past QDRs have drawn harsh criticism from the left and right of the political spectrum, whether deserved or not. Demands for advance screening by Congress, the media, and the defense industry usually result in an anticlimactic unveiling of the report. With the QDR hype building every four years, many reviewers expect dramatic changes to strategies and budgets in response to contemporary events tied to national security. The expectation is that these notable changes manifest themselves in the form of big-ticket program cancellations, shifts between service budgets, and major changes in roles and missions. In fact, many believe the QDR preserves the status quo, drives up the defense budget, and fails to promote healthy service competition to spur transformation—in sum, the QDR process seems to generate consensus between the military services.[3]

The most compelling manifestation of preserving the status quo is evident in the static percentages of service budget share or total obligating authority (TOA) that have remained relatively consistent, despite each QDR. From 1980 to 2006, the US Army's allocation averaged 18 percent of the DOD total investment; from 2007 to 2011, it is projected to decrease to about 17 percent; and from 2012 to 2024, it could grow to about 21 percent. The US Navy and Marine Corps budgets were 34 percent of the DOD's budget from 1980 to 2006; from 2007 to 2011, the budgets dipped by 1 percent to 33 percent; and from 2012 to 2024, they were projected to decrease another 3 percent to 28 percent of the DOD budget. Similarly, the Air Force budget was 38 percent of the DOD total from 1980 to 2006, dipping 3 percent to 35 percent of the total from 2007 to 2011. It is projected to become 40 percent from 2012 to 2024. The stagnant nature of service TOA is more evident when depicted graphically, as in figure 1.[4]

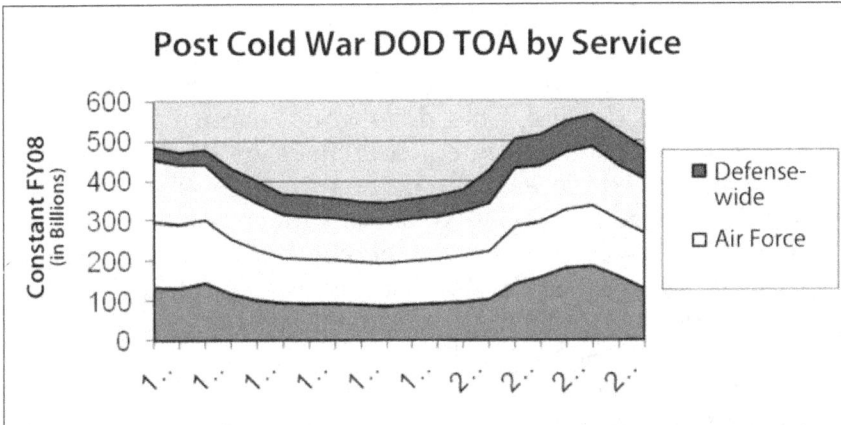

Figure 1. Post-cold-war DOD TOA by service. (Reprinted from DOD Green Book, http://www.defenselink.mil/comptroller/defbudget/fy2009/FY09Green book/greenbook 2009 updated.)

As already stated, the QDR process has failed since 1993 to shake up service budget shares. Since the Gulf War, the nature of the threat has changed. In that time, why have service budget shares not shifted more than a few percentage points? Weapons programs also have become more expensive. The budget grew proportionally for each service, as US defense planning strategy shifted from threat- to capabilities-based, and US national security focus shifted from post–Cold War drift to combating violent extremism. Why hasn't the QDR shaken up service budget shares? The gap between strategy and budget, or ends and means, has only widened as US national defense becomes more complex and expensive.[5]

QDR critics also contend that it merely serves to insure the growth of the defense budget from year to year. They also say the institutional momentum of expensive defense programs, with budgets spread over several administrations, are difficult to cut without significantly impacting related programs and the larger US economy. They proceed to point out that DOD's "un-willingness to reduce . . . big-ticket programs that represent strategic 'dead wood' will see these programs consume ever greater levels of funding in the coming years."[6]

According to the Congressional Budget Office (CBO), DOD's spending grew through the early 1980s. It reached its zenith in 1983, then declined, reaching its nadir in 2000, but then began a steady climb through 2006. However, DOD spending after 2006, as a percentage of the GDP, was projected to show a gradual decline. That drop would occur because projected real (inflation-adjusted) increases in the GDP would outpace projected increases in defense outlays. The CBO projects DOD's share of the GDP to actually decrease to as little as 2.5 percent by 2024.[7] Regardless of whether DOD budgets are compared against the GDP or inflation-adjusted dollars, the QDR process currently has produced neither a definite increase nor decrease in overall DOD budgets.

Another criticism of the QDR is that it fails to encourage the real competition and leader-driven decisions necessary to elicit real change. None of the military branches wants to be accused of attacking another, but each fiercely defends its budget share against that of the other services. An increasing cultural emphasis on service cooperation and joint war fighting is also occurring. Thus, each service builds upon its existing staff and prepares to defend its budget share. Again, as none wants to lose budget share, or appear to surrender budget share, the QDR usually ends in consensus, with only marginal programmatic changes.

In spite of stagnant service shares in the budget and lack of prioritization on defense programs, this study concludes that the QDR process has resulted in important recommendations— as such, the QDR is worthwhile and should not be cancelled. For example, the QDR of 2006 calls for future investment in "key strategic and operational areas, such as persistent surveillance and long-range strike, stealth, operational maneuver and sustainment of air, sea, ground forces at strategic distances, air dominance and undersea warfare."[8] Deputy Secretary of Defense Gordon England stated the QDR of 2006 report was "not a fire-and-forget document" and "will implement" over 100 specific actions.[9]

The QDR of 2006 did not eliminate certain unpopular weapons systems, including the Army's Future Combat Systems, the Navy's DD(X) destroyer, or the Air Force's F-22A. However, it did recommend (1) increasing SOFs by 15 percent (including a 2,600-person Marine component in Special Operations Command), more Navy SEAL capacity and a new Special Operations Command unmanned armored vehicle (UAV) squadron; also (2) expanding psychological operations and civil affairs units by 3,500 personnel and enhancing the capability of the Army and the Marines to perform SOF missions; (3) fielding a new land-based, penetrating long-range strike capability by 2018; accelerating procurement of Predator and Global Hawk UAVs to provide almost double the current UAV coverage; (4) accelerating procurement of Littoral combat ships and developing a Navy riverine capability; (5) fielding a conventional ballistic missile on Trident submarines for conventional prompt global strike; (6) mounting a $1.5 billion initiative to develop broad-spectrum medical countermeasures against the threat of genetically engineered bioterror agents; and (7) advocating a new counterinsurgency (COIN) Air Force long-range strike bomber by 2018. The QDR also discussed COIN doctrine and increases in civilian capacity, stating that "[f]uture warriors will be as proficient in irregular operations, including counterinsurgency and stabilization operations, as they are today in high-intensity combat."[10] These important recommendations represented the potential for long-term change, although carrying the burden of higher budgets without commensurate reductions in other areas. The challenge is to ensure QDR recommendations are continually addressed in the annual PPBE process.

A Quadrennial National Security Review

The Pentagon's PPBE process and the QDR may be two of the best examples of functioning planning processes within the US government's bureaucracy. In this capacity, the DOD could teach the rest of the interagency. Although the QDR suffers from myopia[11] (for fear that massive programmatic changes could cut the defense budget to a point beyond repair), the QDR may be the springboard to help the interagency lengthen and broaden the scope of its thinking and planning. By enlarging the QDR in a time-phased, piecemeal fashion, the entire national security apparatus could become more integrated, efficient, and better at strategic planning.

In the 2005 report, *Beyond Goldwater-Nichols*, Clark Murdock and Michèle Flournoy proposed the enlargement of the QDR to include the broader national security structure, with the National Security Council leading. These two respected analysts called for a review that produces both the National Security Planning Guidance and the unclassified National Security Strategy. Key components would be delineating interagency roles and responsibilities while setting US national security policies and capability requirements. The QNSR would precede and provide context for specific agency reviews like DOD's QDR.[12] The leap to a QNSR, however, is a big one. Congress, DOD, and the interagency are arguably not prepared for that step in the near term. However, Congress recently took a big step by directing the DOD to conduct a roles and missions review. While legislation supporting a quadrennial national security review act was introduced on 26 July 2007, no debate has occurred since, nor has there been a House or Senate vote.[13] Clearly, there exists a desire to conduct a QNSR. Other obstacles preventing *near-term* implementation include the presidential election and associated confirmation hearings and continued management of the conflicts in Iraq and Afghanistan, to name a couple. This long executive and legislative to-do list requires a lot from the DOD and the rest of the interagency.[14] Fixing the QDR from within the DOD may be more attainable before including the rest of the government in the fix.

A Persistent QDR

Three DOD senior leaders and at least one congressman recently promoted developing the QDR as an ongoing process, one that is persistently exercised and monitored for progress.

Donald Rumsfeld felt the QDR should be "a waypoint along a continuum of change,"[15] and Deputy Secretary of Defense England promised that the QDR of 2006 would not be "a fire-and-forget document."[16] Lastly, Ryan Henry, principal deputy undersecretary of defense for Policy and OSD's lead on QDR, states "Past QDRs have taught us that not all decisions can be made within the confines of the formal QDR process; instead it may be necessary to plan to continue work beyond the formal QDR."[17] Instead of ramping up separate QDR staffs for the OSD, joint, and service staffs every four years, the QDR results could gain more traction through a continual process. One such vehicle for implementing a persistent QDR is via the National Defense Panel (NDP), which could provide Congress with an alternative view to that provided by the Pentagon. The NDP would allow a new presidential administration to adjust the QDR, capitalize upon existing Pentagon staffs conducting studies, and generate greater congressional buy-ins. One of the key takeaways from the NDP findings was that the QDR lacked a "strong follow-through" mechanism.

The good news is that there already exists a persistent process in place called PPBE. The problem is that QDR recommendations are not always reflected in the president's budget. If the PPBE processes already in place could be tied to a QDR with built-in off-ramps, more QDR recommendations stand to make it into the budget. The counter argument is that a persistent QDR is merely a way to avoid hard-budget choices, instead the QDR would become a future capabilities showcase without programmatics.[18] In other words, by delaying the hard decisions, the current administration would delay potentially unpopular, hard-to-decide budget cuts, leaving them for a subsequent administration.[19] This paper further explores the concept of a PQDR and recommends it to improve the current process.

Notes

1. Kathleen Hicks and Jim Thomas, interview by authors, 2 October 2007.
2. Flournoy, remarks to the Air Staff, 20 April 2005.
3. Thomas, interview by authors, 26 September 2007.
4. Congressional Budget Office (CBO), "The Long-Term Implications of Current Defense Plans," figure 3-2.
5. Donnelly, "Kill the QDR."

6. Krepinevich, "The Quadrennial Defense Review," 14.

7. CBO, "The Long-Term Implications of Current Defense Plans," figure 1-2. It is also useful to compare DOD budgets through the lens of constant-year (inflation adjusted) dollars. This comparison shows that TOA, in 2007 dollars, grew rapidly between the early and mid-1980s, and reached a peak of $457 billion in 1985. TOA generally declined during the late 1980s and into the 1990s, reaching a low point of about $309 billion in 1997. DOD's TOA began to rise thereafter, reaching $353 billion by 2001. It has grown even more rapidly in recent years as US forces have become engaged in operations in Afghanistan and Iraq. In 2006 DOD's TOA reached $549 billion, including $120 billion to fund those operations ($70 billion in supplemental appropriations and $50 billion provided as part of the Department of Defense Appropriations Act of 2006). If the program in the 2006 FY defense plans was carried out as envisioned and as CBO projected, the demand for defense resources, excluding resources for contingencies, would average $492 billion a year between 2012 and 2024—or about $53 billion more than the 2007 request.

8. DOD, QDR of 2006, 31.

9. Murdock, "An Assessment of the 2006 QDR."

10. DOD, QDR of 2006, 42.

11. Murdock, et al., "Beyond Goldwater-Nichols," 29.

12. Ibid., 79, 85–86.

13. US House 3198: "Quadrennial National Security Review Act," online at http://www.govtrack.us.

14. Hopkins, interview by authors, 18 April 2008.

15. Secretary of Defense Donald H. Rumsfeld, Pentagon Press Conference, 1 February 2006.

16. Deputy Secretary of Defense Gordon England, remarks at event organized by the Center for Strategic and International Studies, 1 February 2006.

17. Henry, "Defense Transformation," 8.

18. Tiron, "Pentagon Strategists Ponder Value of High-Tech Weapons."

19. Flournoy, "Did the Pentagon Get the Quadrennial Defense Review Right?" 67–84.

Chapter 4

Recommendation for Implementing a PQDR

Show me your budget priorities and I'll show you your strategy.

—Unknown

The institutional and organizational momentum of the Pentagon's planning, programming, and budgeting system will continue well into the future. It has worked well and, blended with a PQDR, may be a simple but effective change to defense planning. Therefore, the legislative mandate for the DOD to conduct a continual or persistent QDR should add to the Pentagon's budget-driven processes. This study argues for a QDR process that derives from the good work conducted daily by the DOD. The adoption/implementation of a PQDR will cause fewer perturbations for the DOD and will provide incremental inputs and adjustments for defense strategists and planners. The proposed submission schedule would remain quadrennial. However, Congress will likely welcome the PQDR having experienced a persistent exposure to gradual changes in defense strategy over the previous four years.

Concept and Timing

Realistically, a sitting president has one shot at implementing an agenda into the QDR process. As it currently stands, this opportunity comes during the first six months of his or her administration. These first six months are filled with Senate confirmation of political appointees and setting initial domestic and foreign policy priorities, all superimposed on top of the tyranny of the in-box and the day-to-day business of running the government. When the scope is narrowed to the Department of Defense alone, the next US president will have from Inauguration Day in January 2009 until about the end of the fiscal year in September to set defense budget priorities and to draft a QDR. In the following year, he will focus on implementing guidance for developing the defense force and president's budget execution, which does not allow much time to make a lasting impact that will endure beyond the presidential term. The only continuity between the current and subsequent presidential administrations will likely be the career civil servants. But the QDR should be more than a stand-alone document. Instead of a new president having to either accept or reject the previous document, a PQDR allows for acceptance of those concepts embraced by the next administration (not unlike a line-item veto).

The PQDR would create more time to enact the president's agenda. It could extend this compressed timeline, allowing more opportunities for a new president to make a mark over the entire four-year term. The concept would be to tie the existent PPBE processes to the QDR, creating feedback and accountability. The current QDR is a punctuation mark for the PPBE (fig. 2).

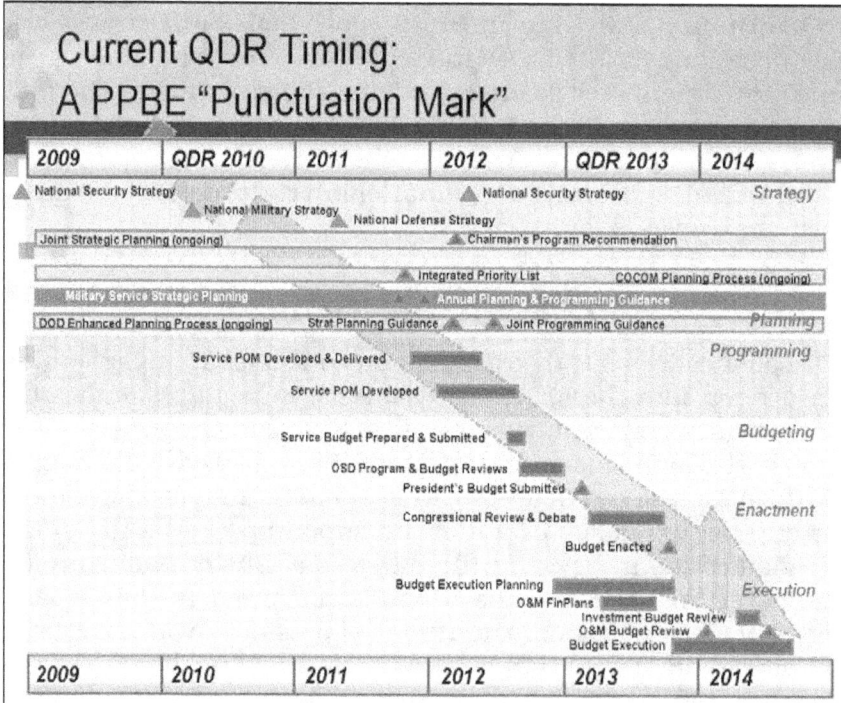

Figure 2. Current QDR timing: A PPBE "punctuation mark." (Reprinted from SAF/FMBP, "Introduction to PPBE [as modified]," April 2007.)

The authors contend that a shortcoming of the PPBE process is that is does not allow for an incremental adjustment or feedback. Contrast this with a proposed four-year process that feeds into the existing planning, programming, and budgeting processes. Based on presidential guidance, one way to combine the two processes would be to create quarterly focus areas that mirror the existing capability portfolios determined by the secretary of defense.

The QDRs of 1997 and 2001 were reported to Congress in September, just before the start of a new fiscal year, and left little time for fiscal adjustments. The QDR of 2006 saw a shift in deadline from September to February of the following year, allowed more than a year after presidential inauguration, and tacked six more months onto the previous deadline. This put the QDR suspense in line more closely with the defense budget submission.[1] By extending the deadline, incoming presidents have more time to address their particular defense strategy concerns. The alignment of QDR and budget submissions also lend to a better translation from strategy to cost—a step in the right direction.

Structure and Content

In the authors' estimation, the PQDR should be limited in scope. It should not be a soup-to-nuts exercise but should focus on a collection of the most important strategic initiatives.[2] Under this construct, the various DOD staffs would focus on a handful of carefully chosen areas, as driven by the secretary of defense. Of course, future QDR development teams also will have to fight the temptation of drafting overly ambitious goals or terms of reference. Past QDRs fought the competing priority of becoming overly narrow or broad. The four core challenges of the QDR of 2006 were initially faulted as being narrow, while the terms of reference were thought to be ambitious.[3]

The PQDR should not be a budget-cut drill. Although previous reviews have been constrained by fiscal guidance, the PQDR should require that specific offsets should accompany any recommended increases.[4]

The PQDR should attempt to balance risk through structured competition. The QDR of 2001, for example, set out to balance four categories of risk: force management, operational, future challenge, and institutional.[5] Such a finite set of competing priorities would vie for relative fair shares of a limited defense budget. The PQDR would incorporate such a group of priorities consistently throughout the four-year effort.

The design and rhythm of a proposed PQDR would be relatively straightforward. On a quarterly basis, OSD and JCS should consider a new secretary of defense–chosen focus area, as defined at the outset of each presidential administration. The QDR teams would then embark on a series of expert panel discussions and war games designed to challenge conventional thinking on that particular topic. The PQDR would thus be a bottom-up process with a top-down agenda and accountability.

The PQDR should also include a roles and functions study (appendix C).[6] On 25 July 2007 the House Armed Services Committee announced the creation of a committee panel to examine the roles and missions of the military services. Congress recognized that the DOD had not conducted a serious study of traditional service roles and missions since the late 1940s. Because roles and missions are so closely related to defense strategy and budgets, it makes sense to tie this new congressional reporting requirement into the PQDR process.

The PQDR will capitalize on other existing DOD processes. Aside from PPBE, the capability portfolio managers (appendix D) and Execution Road Map Studies should tie into the PQDR. In conjunction with the QDR of 2006, nine execution road map groups were established to focus on topics to guide the six-year plan for investment and organization from 2008 to 2013. Two cochairs should be assigned to lead each group. One of them should be a senior OSD civilian and the other a senior military officer from either the Joint Staff or a joint command. The execution road maps could be overseen by the DAWG, made up of the deputy defense secretary, vice chairman of the JCS, and the service vice chiefs. The execution road maps should appear in the program objective memorandum (POM) of 2008. It is expected that only those groups with a more programmatic focus will really influence the POM.[7] Of note, the DOD has since organized capability portfolio managers who are charged with integrating and long-range planning of nine specific defense functions. The hope is that such constructs lead to long-term corporate memory and cross-leveling of redundant service capabilities. The existing OSD capability portfolios could serve as PQDR focus area templates. A handful of the capability portfolios could be addressed quarterly—at a rate of two or three per quarter. Capacity would be left during each quarter to address items outside the existing portfolio sets. In contrast to figure 2, figure 3 depicts essentially 16 opportunities (one per quarter) over four years to adjust and inject changes to the QDR.

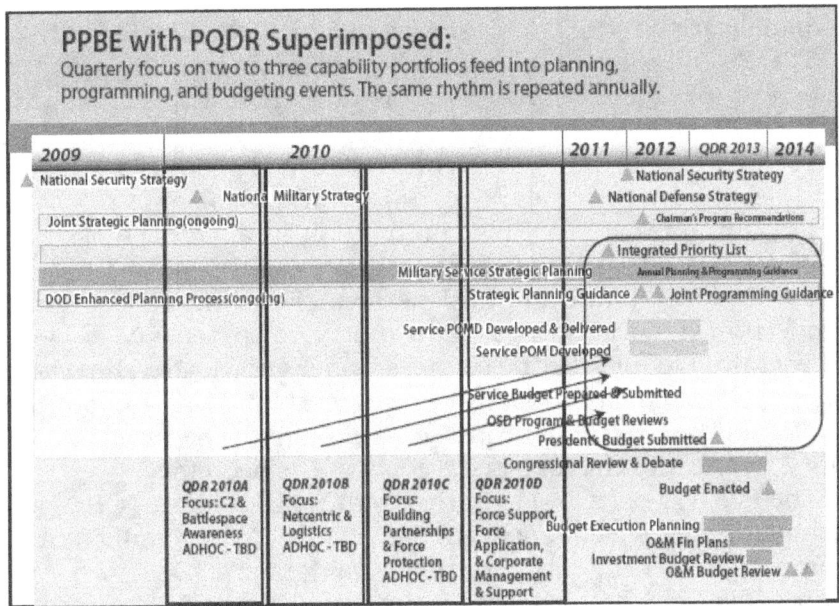

Figure 3. Current PPBE with PQDR superimposed. (Reprinted from SAF/FMBP, "Introduction to PPBE [as modified]," April 2008.)

Leadership and Competition

The secretary of defense would name the quarterly focus areas—a top-down approach. Ongoing DOD war games, analyses, red teaming, and modeling would be tailored to coincide with a given quarterly focus area. The QDR, as PQDR, would become "highly iterative and [could] include an assessment of each of these scenario's individual demands . . . [examining] the stresses placed on U.S. forces when scenarios are confronted in different combinations."[8] This process would add objective credibility to purported capabilities requirements. Successful *routine* use of this approach would encourage the DOD leadership to adopt an analytical, scenario-based paradigm to use in risk and trade-off analyses.[9] By using existing staffs, with senior direction on the themes and context of military war games, the QDR could be revised on a quarterly basis. This would keep the staff focused on senior leader goals, provide Congress a more informed assessment of the DOD's future, and offer a new presidential administration more opportunities to adjust the DOD's path.

The PQDR also would hold the services accountable to the secretary of defense's priorities. As one might expect, the primary obstacle to change will be related to service budgets. With CBO predictions that service budgets are expected to level off and decline by 2010, the services are likely to "dig in" as the next QDR approaches. This could result in a sacrifice of modernization programs as legacy programs hold fast, or the converse as older platforms and personnel are traded for more modern systems. The execution road map process was carefully crafted to include the services under OSD leadership oversight. The intended impact will be to lend longevity to both the QDR and the road map processes, enabling the services to continue to execute the long-term goals of the secretary.[10]

The PQDR would reside in the Joint Staff (J-8) and OSD policy planning, special operations, low-intensity conflict, and comptroller. These organizations hold past QDR corporate knowledge and presently house many of the QDR processes. Chiefly, these include strategy, planning, and budget. At the same time, the services will maintain PQDR staffs in their respective planning and budgeting organizations, traditionally, the G-8 and the A-8. This differs from past practices where the services have expanded staff capacity with added contractor support in the months preceding QDR planning efforts. Under a PQDR, the services would be forced to maintain a QDR staff to conduct ongoing studies that culminate every four years as a congressional QDR report.[11]

The PQDR will allow more dialogue with the service chiefs. While the services keep their QDR staffs employed throughout the four-year reporting cycle, two particular challenges emerge.

The first will be to empower the service chiefs to express their views, independent of the chairman, without taking away from the chairman's role as principal advisor to the president and the secretary of defense. While the views of the chiefs must be considered, some caution is warranted. Every service has a culture and cultural bias to accompany it. In the case of the generals and admirals, it's an insistence not so much on expensive weapons as on particular kinds of expensive weapons. For the Air Force, this means more tactical fighter planes, while the Navy presses for more carriers and submarines. This pattern may persist, as these capabilities represent frontline weapon systems associated with these services.[12]

Outreach and Partnering

The PQDR should include international partners in the process. US defense planning must reach out to engage with likely coalition nations. Indeed, several of the United States' closest international allies and partners helped to develop the defense review of 2006. Military officers from some of America's closest allies, including Canada, the United Kingdom, and Australia, participated in a series of high-level roundtable discussions where each of the four core partners and their representatives also were integrated into the QDR staff. The PQDR should expand consultations to include such allies as Japan, France, and Germany.[13] In the past, OSD also consulted with representatives from the United Kingdom, Canada, Australia, Italy, the Netherlands, Germany, Sweden, Poland, Singapore, Japan, Korea, and India, as well as the North Atlantic Treaty Organization.[14] This practice should be continued.

The PQDR also needs a political strategy. Specifically, it needs participation from key members and committees on Capitol Hill. For starters, it should include a regular consultation process with the chairs and ranking members of the key defense committees in the Senate and the House of Representatives.[15] Failing to do so could yield a level of mistrust and doubt, causing the Congress to embark on its own congressional defense review.[16]

Thus, the PQDR would build a stronger relationship between the OSD and the Congress. Every change in the OSD budget priorities potentially impacts dollars flowing to specific congressional district(s). If a QDR recommendation results in unpopular budget decisions, its chance of success may be marginalized. However, if the nature of the QDR is transformed as proposed, an opportunity for incremental change presents itself, lessening the chances for surprise program cuts. In other words, bad news does not get better with age. A good example is the controversy over Air Force airlift aircraft. Congress would like both to extend the life of the C-5 and to buy more new C-17s. The Air Force prefers the latter, wanting newer, more reliable platforms. With longer exposure to the problem, Congress has the opportunity to adjust and buy into proposed program modifications, possibly resulting in a maximized acquisition versus a convenient one.[17]

The PQDR should result in a new planning horizon in Congress. Instead of only focusing on the traditional one-to-five-year PPBE horizon with a 20-year look into the future, the PQDR integrated with DOD's PPBE will take a slightly different approach. These changes would result in three new timelines: 20-, 10-, and five-year developing plans for each horizon. Programming and budgeting would also follow suit, using the same intervals. The traditional five-year planning horizon would be adjusted on a quarterly basis. For the 10-year planning horizon, the process would be repeated every two years; while the longer 20-year planning horizon would occur every five to 10 years.

Notes

1. Osowski, "Approaching the QDR as a Process."

2. Flournoy, remarks, "Goldwater-Nichols."

3. Flournoy, "Did the Pentagon Get the Quadrennial Defense Review Right?" 67–84.

4. Ratman, "QDR May Devolve into a Budget-Cutting Recipe," 6.

5. McKenzie, Jr., "Assessing Risk: Enabling Sound Defense Decisions," 193–216.

6. US House Armed Services Committee Roles and Missions Panel, "Initial Perspectives," January 2008. Functions date from Pres. Harry S. Truman's 1947 executive order on the "Functions of the Armed Forces." They include those various activities, operations, and capabilities for which the services are responsible and for which they were charged with the "organizing, training, and equipping" of combat-ready forces. Missions belong to specified and

unified combatant commanders, formerly called commanders in chiefs. In the context of this paper, roles are associated with the services, while missions are used in the context of intelligence agencies, State Department, the National Security Council, and other agencies in protecting American security.

7. Osowski, "Approaching the QDR as a Process."

8. Flournoy, "Did the Pentagon Get the Quadrennial Defense Review Right?" 67–84.

9. Ibid., 67–84.

10. Osowski, "Approaching the QDR as a Process."

11. Lisa Disbrow, interview notes, 16 October 2007.

12. Kaplan, "Rumsfeld Surrender."

13. Jim Thomas, interview by authors, 26 September 2007.

14. Flournoy, "Did the Pentagon Get the Quadrennial Defense Review Right?" 67–84.

15. Thomas, interview notes, 26 September 2007.

16. House, Committee on Armed Services, "CDR: Fact Sheet," 13.

17. Osowski, "Approaching the QDR as a Process."

Chapter 5

Conclusion

At the end of the day, much of the strategy was lost somewhere in translation.

—Michèle A. Flournoy, on the QDR of 2006

After the QDR of 2006 was released, the US Air Force cut its end-strength by 40,000, the US Marine Corps added 27,000, and the Army grew by 56,000 personnel. These major force structure changes did not grow from QDR recommendations. Aside from established PPBE processes, how could major force structure changes have happened outside the QDR process, albeit during wartime? The QDR process should provide for regular off-ramps or opportunities to adjust.

Note that Congress passed legislation that added new reporting elements for the next QDR in 2010 and for future QDRs. For example, under current rules, the secretary of defense must establish an independent panel to conduct a post-review assessment of the QDR, including the recommendations, assumptions used, and vulnerabilities of the strategy and force structure underlying the review. New legislation also required that the secretary of defense submit to the Senate and the House Committees on Armed Services quarterly reports on the status of the department's implementation of the QDR 2006 decisions.[1]

A successful QDR requires the buy in not only of the senior civilian leadership of the department but also that of others, including the military leaders who will have to implement it and the members of Congress who will ultimately vote on the administration's budget submissions.[2] A process that occurs once every four years has thus far failed to produce the lofty goals set out at the outset of past QDRs. An incremental, continuous process could keep the debate open, allowing for periodic change and adjustment.

The last QDR left the DOD equipped mainly for prosecuting successful traditional warfare. Examples include the Army's future combat system, the Navy's DD(X) destroyer, the Air

Forces' F-35 fighter, and the Marine Corp's V-22 transport aircraft. The future combat system, projected to cost more than $150 billion, was conceived to exploit information technologies to defeat traditional challenges—an area of declining competition. The DD(X) destroyer, at roughly $4 billion for the first ship in the class, is a firepower platform. Yet, it may be irrelevant in addressing an undersea challenge from China. The F-35 fighter, the most expensive program in the defense budget at over $250 billion, is designed to be both a fighter and ground attack aircraft. In contrast, some believe the most worrisome rival strike systems being fielded require a counter to ballistic and cruise missiles. The V-22 aircraft, designed to hover like a helicopter and fly like a plane, has become so expensive that it may not be built in large enough numbers to deliver the necessary wartime mass to make a difference.[3] The US military needs to maintain its conventional war-fighting superiority, but it also needs to reduce its investment in capabilities that simply expand its margin of conventional superiority to free up resources that will improve US war-fighting capabilities across the spectrum of conflict.[4] Thus far, it appears that the QDR has failed to adequately translate some future battlefield requirements into programmatic realities.

Some critics of the QDR process also argue that the big bang approach to defense transformation doesn't work. In other words, transforming the DOD can only be done one big decision at a time through a robust strategic-planning process that ties up strategic choices for the leadership and enables them to make decisions that establish the strategic direction of the department.[5] The notion of a persistent QDR opens the door for the secretary of defense to make incremental muscle movements. The PQDR would provide a series of data sets allowing gradual programmatic adjustments in light of long-range strategy, with feedback opportunities built-in into the planning, programming, and budgeting cycle. The strength of this recommended approach lies in its timing. The review would not materialize solely because of an election, although this will be a primary driver of change. Instead, it would be based on the need to continuously re-focus US military plans and investments in response to changing international context and presidential prerogatives. Future related studies should examine the mechanisms required to implement a quadrennial national security review across the entire national security enterprise.

Notes

1. GAO, "John Warner National Defense Authorization Act for Fiscal Year 2007," 3.

2. Flournoy, remarks to the Air Staff, 20 April 2005.

3. Krepinevich, "Quadrennial Defense Review," 10.

4. Flournoy, "Did the Pentagon Get the Quadrennial Defense Review Right?" 67–84.

5. Murdock, correspondence with Michèle Flournoy, 29 December 2005, in Flournoy, "Did the Pentagon Get the Quadrennial Defense Review Right?" 67–84.

Appendix A

Legislation Pertaining
to QDR Establishment

H.R. 3230

National Defense Authorization Act for Fiscal Year 1997
(Enrolled Bill [Sent to President])
Subtitle B—Force Structure Review

SEC. 921. SHORT TITLE.

This subtitle may be cited as the 'Military Force Structure Review Act of 1996'.

SEC. 922. FINDINGS.

Congress makes the following findings:

(1) Since the collapse of the Soviet Union in 1991, the United States has conducted two substantial assessments of the force structure of the Armed Forces necessary to meet United States defense requirements.

(2) The assessment by the Bush Administration (known as the 'Base Force' assessment) and the assessment by the Clinton Administration (known as the 'Bottom-Up Review') were intended to reassess the force structure of the Armed Forces in light of the changing realities of the post–Cold War world.

(3) Both assessments served an important purpose in focusing attention on the need to reevaluate the military posture of the United States, but the pace of global change necessitates a new, comprehensive assessment of the defense strategy of the United States and the force structure of the Armed Forces required to meet the threats to the United States in the twenty-first century.

(4) The Bottom-Up Review has been criticized on several points, including—

(A) The assumptions underlying the strategy of planning to fight and win two nearly simultaneous major regional conflicts;

(B) The force levels recommended to carry out that strategy; and

(C) The funding proposed for such recommended force levels.

(5) In response to the recommendations of the Commission on Roles and Missions of the Armed Forces, the Secretary of Defense endorsed the concept of conducting a quadrennial review of the defense program at the beginning of each newly elected Presidential administration, and the Department intends to complete the first such review in 1997.

(6) The review is to involve a comprehensive examination of defense strategy, the force structure of the active, guard, and reserve components, force modernization plans, infrastructure, and other elements of the defense program and policies in order to determine and express the defense strategy of the United States and to establish a revised defense program through the year 2005.

(7) In order to ensure that the force structure of the Armed Forces is adequate to meet the challenges to the national security interests of the United States in the twenty-first century, to assist the Secretary of Defense in conducting the review referred to in paragraph (5), and to assess the appropriate force structure of the Armed Forces through the year 2010 and beyond (if practicable), it is important to provide for the conduct of an independent, nonpartisan review of the force structure that is more comprehensive than prior assessments of the force structure, extends beyond the quadrennial defense review, and explores innovative and forward-thinking ways of meeting such challenges.

SEC. 923. QUADRENNIAL DEFENSE REVIEW.

(a) REQUIREMENT IN 1997- The Secretary of Defense, in consultation with the Chairman of the Joint Chiefs of Staff, shall complete in 1997 a review of the defense program of the United States intended to satisfy the requirements for a Quadrennial Defense Review as identified in the recommendations of the Commission on Roles and Missions of the Armed Forces. The review shall include a comprehensive examination of the defense strategy, force structure, force modernization plans, infrastructure, budget plan, and other elements of the defense program and policies with a view toward determining and expressing the defense strategy of the United States and establishing a revised defense program through the year 2005.

(b) INVOLVEMENT OF NATIONAL DEFENSE PANEL-

(1) The Secretary shall apprise the National Defense Panel established under section 924, on an ongoing basis, of the work undertaken in the conduct of the review.

(2) Not later than March 14, 1997, the Chairman of the National Defense Panel shall submit to the Secretary the Panel's assessment of work undertaken in the conduct of the review as of that date and shall include in the assessment the recommendations of the Panel for improvements to the review, including recommendations for additional matters to be covered in the review.

(c) ASSESSMENTS OF REVIEW- Upon completion of the review, the Chairman of the Joint Chiefs of Staff and the Chairman of the National Defense Panel, on behalf of the Panel, shall each prepare and submit to the Secretary such Chairman's assessment of the review in time for the inclusion of the assessment in its entirety in the report under subsection (d).

(d) REPORT- Not later than May 15, 1997, the Secretary shall submit to the Committee on Armed Services of the Senate and the Committee on National Security of the House of Representatives a comprehensive report on the review. The report shall include the following:

(1) The results of the review, including a comprehensive discussion of the defense strategy of the United States and the force structure best suited to implement that strategy.

(2) The threats examined for purposes of the review and the scenarios developed in the examination of such threats.

(3) The assumptions used in the review, including assumptions relating to the cooperation of allies and mission-sharing, levels of acceptable risk, warning times, and intensity and duration of conflict.

(4) The effect on the force structure of preparations for and participation in peace operations and military operations other than war.

(5) The effect on the force structure of the utilization by the Armed Forces of technologies anticipated to be available by the year 2005, including precision guided munitions, stealth, night vision, digitization, and communications, and the changes in doctrine and operational concepts that would result from the utilization of such technologies.

(6) The manpower and sustainment policies required under the defense strategy to support engagement in conflicts lasting more than 120 days.

(7) The anticipated roles and missions of the reserve components in the defense strategy and the strength, capabilities, and equipment necessary to assure that the reserve components can capably discharge those roles and missions.

(8) The appropriate ratio of combat forces to support forces (commonly referred to as the 'tooth-to-tail' ratio) under the defense strategy, including, in particular, the appropriate number and size of headquarter units and Defense Agencies for that purpose.

(9) The air-lift and sea-lift capabilities required to support the defense strategy.

(10) The forward presence, pre-positioning, and other anticipatory deployments necessary under the defense strategy for conflict deterrence and adequate military response to anticipated conflicts.

(11) The extent to which resources must be shifted among two or more theaters under the defense strategy in the event of conflict in such theaters.

(12) The advisability of revisions to the Unified Command Plan as a result of the defense strategy.

(13) Any other matter the Secretary considers appropriate.

Appendix B

Public Law Pertaining to the QDR

10 USC Sec. 118   01/02/2006

-EXPCITE-

TITLE 10 - ARMED FORCES

Subtitle A - General Military Law

PART I - ORGANIZATION AND GENERAL MILITARY POWERS

CHAPTER 2 - DEPARTMENT OF DEFENSE

-HEAD-

Sec. 118. Quadrennial defense review

-STATUTE-

(a) Review Required. - The Secretary of Defense shall every four years, during a year following a year evenly divisible by four, conduct a comprehensive examination (to be known as a "quadrennial defense review") of the national defense strategy, force structure, force modernization plans, infrastructure, budget plan, and other elements of the defense program and policies of the United States with a view toward determining and expressing the defense strategy of the United States and establishing a defense program for the next 20 years. Each such quadrennial defense review shall be conducted in consultation with the Chairman of the Joint Chiefs of Staff.

(b) Conduct of Review. - Each quadrennial defense review shall be conducted so as -

(1) to delineate a national defense strategy consistent with the most recent National Security Strategy prescribed by the President pursuant to section 108 of the National Security Act of 1947 (50 U.S.C. 404a);

(2) to define sufficient force structure, force modernization plans, infrastructure, budget plan, and other elements of the defense program of the United States associated with that national defense strategy that would be required to execute successfully the full range of missions called for in that national defense strategy; and

(3) to identify (A) the budget plan that would be required to provide sufficient resources to execute successfully the full range of missions called for in that national defense strategy at a low-to-moderate level of risk, and (B) any additional resources (beyond those programmed in the current future-years defense program) required to achieve such a level of risk.

(c) Assessment of Risk. - The assessment of risk for the purposes of subsection (b) shall be undertaken by the Secretary of Defense in consultation with the Chairman of the Joint Chiefs of Staff. That assessment shall define the nature and magnitude of the political, strategic, and military risks associated with executing the missions called for under the national defense strategy.

(d) Submission of QDR to Congressional Committees. – The Secretary shall submit a report on each quadrennial defense review to the Committees on Armed Services of the Senate and the House of Representatives. The report shall be submitted in the year following the year in which the review is conducted, but not later than the date on which the President submits the budget for the next fiscal year to Congress under section 1105(a) of title 31. The report shall include the following:

(1) The results of the review, including a comprehensive discussion of the national defense strategy of the United States and the force structure best suited to implement that strategy at a low-to-moderate level of risk.

(2) The assumed or defined national security interests of the United States that inform the national defense strategy defined in the review.

(3) The threats to the assumed or defined national security interests of the United States that were examined for the purposes of the review and the scenarios developed in the examination of those threats.

(4) The assumptions used in the review, including assumptions relating to -

(A) the status of readiness of United States forces;

(B) the cooperation of allies, mission-sharing and additional benefits to and burdens on United States forces resulting from coalition operations;

(C) warning times;

(D) levels of engagement in operations other than war and smaller-scale contingencies and withdrawal from such operations and contingencies; and

(E) the intensity, duration, and military and political end-states of conflicts and smaller-scale contingencies.

(5) The effect on the force structure and on readiness for high-intensity combat of preparations for and participation in operations other than war and smaller-scale contingencies.

(6) The manpower and sustainment policies required under the national defense strategy to support engagement in conflicts lasting longer than 120 days.

(7) The anticipated roles and missions of the reserve components in the national defense strategy and the strength, capabilities, and equipment necessary to assure that the reserve components can capably discharge those roles and missions.

(8) The appropriate ratio of combat forces to support forces (commonly referred to as the "tooth-to-tail" ratio) under the national defense strategy, including, in particular, the appropriate number and size of headquarters units and Defense Agencies for that purpose.

(9) The strategic and tactical air-lift, sea-lift, and ground transportation capabilities required to support the national defense strategy.

(10) The forward presence, pre-positioning, and other anticipatory deployments necessary under the national defense strategy for conflict deterrence and adequate military response to anticipated conflicts.

(11) The extent to which resources must be shifted among two or more theaters under the national defense strategy in the event of conflict in such theaters.

(12) The advisability of revisions to the Unified Command Plan as a result of the national defense strategy.

(13) The effect on force structure of the use by the armed forces of technologies anticipated to be available for the ensuing 20 years.

(14) The national defense mission of the Coast Guard.

(15) Any other matter the Secretary considers appropriate.

(e) CJCS Review. - (1) Upon the completion of each review under subsection (a), the Chairman of the Joint Chiefs of Staff shall prepare and submit to the Secretary of Defense the Chairman's assessment of the review, including the Chairman's assessment of risk.

(2) The Chairman shall include as part of that assessment the Chairman's assessment of the assignment of functions (or roles and missions) to the armed forces, together with any recommendations for changes in assignment that the Chairman considers necessary to achieve maximum efficiency of the armed forces. In preparing the assessment under this paragraph, the Chairman shall consider (among other matters) the following:

(A) Unnecessary duplication of effort among the armed forces.

(B) Changes in technology that can be applied effectively to warfare.

(3) The Chairman's assessment shall be submitted to the Secretary in time for the inclusion of the assessment in the report. The Secretary shall include the Chairman's assessment, together with the Secretary's comments, in the report in its entirety.

-SOURCE-

(Added) Pub. L. 106-65, div. A, title IX, Sec. 901(a)(1), Oct. 5, 1999, 113 Stat. 715; amended Pub. L. 107-107, div. A, title IX, Sec. 921(a), Dec. 28, 2001, 115 Stat. 1198; Pub. L. 107-314, div. A, title IX, Secs. 922, 923, Dec. 2, 2002, 116 Stat. 2623.)

-MISC1-

PRIOR PROVISIONS

A prior section 118, added Pub. L. 97-295, Sec. 1(2)(A), Oct. 12, 1982, 96 Stat. 1288, Sec. 133b; renumbered Sec. 118, Pub. L. 99- 433, title I, Sec. 101(a)(2), Oct. 1, 1986, 100 Stat. 994, required reports to Congress on sales or transfers of defense articles, prior to repeal by Pub. L. 101-510, div. A, title XIII, Sec. 1301(2), Nov. 5, 1990, 104 Stat. 1668.

AMENDMENTS

2002 - Subsec. (d). Pub. L. 107-314, Sec. 922, substituted "in the year following the year in which the review is conducted, but not later than the date on which the President submits the budget for the next fiscal year to Congress under section 1105(a) of title 31" for "not later than September 30 of the year in which the review is conducted" in second sentence of introductory provisions.

Subsec. (d)(14), (15). Pub. L. 107-314, Sec. 923, added par. (14) and redesignated former par. (14) as (15).

2001 - Subsec. (e). Pub. L. 107-107 designated the first sentence of existing provisions as par. (1), the second and third sentences of existing provisions as par. (3), and added par. (2).

-TRANS-

TRANSFER OF FUNCTIONS

For transfer of authorities, functions, personnel, and assets of the Coast Guard, including the authorities and functions of the Secretary of Transportation relating thereto, to the Department of Homeland Security, and for treatment of related references, see sections 468(b), 551(d), 552(d), and 557 of Title 6, Domestic Security, and the Department of Homeland Security Reorganization Plan of November 25, 2002, as modified, set out as a note under section 542 of Title 6.

-MISC2-

ASSESSMENT WITH RESPECT TO 2001 QDR

Pub. L. 107-107, div. A, title IX, Sec. 921(c), Dec. 28, 2001, 115 Stat. 1198, provided that: "With respect to the 2001 Quadrennial Defense Review, the Chairman of the Joint Chiefs of Staff shall submit to Congress a separate assessment of functions (or roles and missions) of the Armed Forces in accordance with paragraph (2) of section 118(e) of title 10, United States Code, as added by subsection (a)(3). Such assessment shall be based on the findings in the 2001 Quadrennial Defense Review, issued by the Secretary of Defense on September 30, 2001, and shall be submitted to Congress not later than one year after the date of the enactment of this Act [Dec. 28, 2001]."

REVISED NUCLEAR POSTURE REVIEW

Pub. L. 106-398, Sec. 1 [[div. A], title X, Sec. 1041], Oct. 30, 2000, 114 Stat. 1654, 1654A-262, as amended by Pub. L. 107-107, div. A, title X, Sec. 1033, Dec. 28, 2001, 115 Stat. 1216, provided that:

(a) Requirement for Comprehensive Review. - In order to clarify United States nuclear deterrence policy and strategy for the near term, the Secretary of Defense shall conduct a comprehensive review of the nuclear posture of the United States for the next 5 to 10 years. The Secretary shall conduct the review in consultation with the Secretary of Energy.

(b) Elements of Review. - The nuclear posture review shall include the following elements:

(1) The role of nuclear forces in United States military strategy, planning, and programming.

(2) The policy requirements and objectives for the United States to maintain a safe, reliable, and credible nuclear deterrence posture.

(3) The relationship among United States nuclear deterrence policy, targeting strategy, and arms control objectives.

(4) The levels and composition of the nuclear delivery systems that will be required for implementing the United States national and military strategy, including any plans for replacing or modifying existing systems.

(5) The nuclear weapons complex that will be required for implementing the United States national and military strategy, including any plans to modernize or modify the complex.

(6) The active and inactive nuclear weapons stockpile that will be required for implementing the United States national and military strategy, including any plans for replacing or modifying warheads.

(7) The possibility of deactivating or de-alerting nuclear warheads or delivery systems immediately, or immediately after a decision to retire any specific warhead, class of warheads, or delivery system.

(c) Report to Congress. - The Secretary of Defense shall submit to Congress, in unclassified and classified forms as necessary, a report on the results of the nuclear posture review conducted under this section. The report shall be submitted concurrently with the Quadrennial Defense Review report due in December 2001.

(d) Sense of Congress. - It is the sense of Congress that the nuclear posture review conducted under this section should be used as the basis for establishing future United States arms control objectives and negotiating positions."

SPECIFIED MATTER FOR NEXT QDR

Pub. L. 106-65, div. A, title IX, Sec. 901(c), Oct. 5, 1999, 113 Stat. 717, provided that: "In the first quadrennial defense review conducted under section 118 of title 10, United States Code, as added by subsection (a), the Secretary shall include in the technologies considered for the purposes of paragraph (13) of subsection (d) of that section the following: precision guided munitions, stealth, night vision, digitization, and communications."

Appendix C

Congressional Roles and Missions Panel

SKELTON AND HUNTER ANNOUNCE
ROLES AND MISSIONS PANEL

Washington, DC – House Armed Services Committee Chairman Ike Skelton (D-MO) and Ranking Member Duncan Hunter (R-CA) announced the creation of a committee panel to examine the roles and missions of the military services. The following members have been named to serve on the Roles and Missions Panel:

Congressman Jim Cooper (D-TN), Chairman
Congressman Rick Larsen (D-WA)
Congresswoman Kristen Gillibrand (D-NY)
Congressman Joe Sestak (D-PA)

Congressman Phil Gingrey (R-GA), Ranking Member
Congressman Geoff Davis (R-KY)
Congressman Michael Conaway (R-TX)

"The basic structure of the Department of Defense and the division of labor between the military services has not dramatically changed since the late 1940s. Ensuring that the military services are working on the appropriate roles and missions is key to our national security and Congress has an important role to play in this effort. Under the able leadership of Chairman Jim Cooper and Ranking Member Phil Gingrey, we will evaluate and identify options in order to maintain the fighting force our nation needs to protect the American people," said Chairman Skelton.

"We look forward to working with our colleagues on this important issue. The assignment of roles and missions to the Armed Services has always been a critical element to America's security. I'd like to thank Rep. Gingrey, Rep. Conaway, Rep. Davis and all of the other members of the panel for agreeing to undertake this important endeavor," said Ranking Member Hunter.

"The military finds itself facing unpredictable threats in a dangerous new world. Our military services have responded bravely to these challenges and are completing missions they never anticipated. This panel will explore the changing missions of the military services, identify gaps in our capabilities, and propose options that ensure the United States can defend itself against every threat to national security. I look forward to beginning this important work with my colleagues," said Congressman Cooper.

"This panel will allow us the opportunity to study an issue vital to our nation's Armed Forces. I am honored to serve as Ranking Member of the panel, and look forward to working together with Chairman Cooper and other panel Members on this important undertaking," said Congressman Gingrey.

Appendix D

OSD Capability Portfolio Guidance, Part 1

DEPUTY SECRETARY OF DEFENSE
1010 DEFENSE PENTAGON
WASHINGTON, DC 20301-1010

FEB - 7 2008

MEMORANDUM FOR SECRETARIES OF THE MILITARY DEPARTMENTS
CHAIRMAN OF THE JOINT CHIEFS OF STAFF
UNDER SECRETARIES OF DEFENSE
CHIEFS OF THE MILITARY SERVICES
COMMANDERS OF THE COMBATANT COMMANDS
ASSISTANT SECRETARIES OF DEFENSE
GENERAL COUNSEL OF THE DEPARTMENT OF DEFENSE
DIRECTOR, OPERATIONAL TEST AND EVALUATION
INSPECTOR GENERAL OF THE DEPARTMENT OF DEFENSE
ASSISTANTS TO THE SECRETARY OF DEFENSE
DIRECTOR, ADMINISTRATION AND MANAGEMENT
DIRECTOR, PROGRAM ANALYSIS AND EVALUATION
DIRECTOR, NET ASSESSMENT
DIRECTORS OF THE DEFENSE AGENCIES
DIRECTORS OF THE DOD FIELD ACTIVITIES

SUBJECT: Capability Portfolio Management Way Ahead

In September 2006, we began to experiment with Capability Portfolio Management. The first four Capability Portfolio Managers (CPMs) participated in the FY09 budget review and prepared force development guidance for FY10, helping the Department make investment decisions; because of this, they will now be formalized as standing CPMs.

In addition to formalizing the four test case CPMs, we will experiment with the remaining five CPMs through the FY10 budget review cycle. Following this, we will determine if these five CPMs should also be formalized.

The matrix below outlines the initial civilian and military leads for each of the nine CPMs and organizations associated with each. We will leverage the expertise of Senior Warfighters Forums (SWarF) to provide operational proponency to their respective portfolios. Functional Capability Boards and Joint Staff offices, as designated by CJCS, will support and participate in CPM activities.

OSD 01824-08

2/8/2008 8:43:54 AM

OSD Capability Portfolio Guidance, Part 2

Capability Portfolio	CPM Civilian Lead	CPM Military Lead	CPM JS OPR	Functional Capability Boards	SWARF Lead
Command & Control (1)	ASD(NII)	JFCOM	J3	JFCOM	JFCOM
Battlespace Awareness (1)	USD(I)	STRATCOM	J2	J2	STRATCOM
Net Centric (1)	ASD(NII)	STRATCOM	J6	J6	STRATCOM
Logistics (1)	USD(AT&L)	TRANSCOM	J4	J4	TRANSCOM
Building Partnerships (2)	USD(P)	J5		J5	JFCOM
Force Protection (2)	USD(AT&L)	J8		J8	STRATCOM
Force Support (2)	USD(P&R)	J8		J8	JFCOM
Force Application (2)	USD (AT&L) USD(P)	JROC	J8	J8	JFCOM SOCOM STRATCOM
Corporate Management & Support (2)	D,A&M	DJS		DJS	N/A

[1] Formal CPM
[2] Experimental CPM

The CPMs make recommendations to the Deputy Secretary of Defense and the Deputy's Advisory Working Group (DAWG) on capability development issues within their respective portfolio. They have no independent decision-making authority and will not infringe on any existing statutory authorities, but they will have access to information and processes required to advise the DAWG. In essence, CPMs integrate, coordinate, and synchronize portfolio content by providing strategic advice intended to focus portfolio capabilities.

The success of Capability Portfolio Management will require cooperation from all participants. The DAWG will receive regular updates on their progress in preparation for, and throughout, the FY10 budget review process.

Appendix E

Potential QDR Service Priorities (Marine Corps and Air Force)

US Marine Corps. According to Department of Defense Directive (DODD) 5100.1, 1 August 2002, the United States Marines Corps shall be organized, trained, and equipped to provide Fleet Marine Forces of combined arms, together with supporting air components, for service with the fleet in the seizure or defense of advanced naval bases and for the conduct of such land operations as may be essential to the prosecution of a naval campaign. In addition, the Marine Corps shall provide organizations for service on US Naval vessels, provide security detachments at naval stations and bases, and perform such other duties directed by the President or the Secretary of Defense.

It is not hard to imagine the Marine Corps as continuing its role as the Nation's 9-1-1 Force: "the Nation's most ready when the Nation is least ready." In order to ensure the Marines remain that Force, its relationship with the United States Navy must continue to be strong. The recent release of the maritime strategy entitled, "A Cooperative Strategy for 21st Century Seapower" (signed by General Conway, commandant of the Marine Corps; Admiral Roughead, chief of Naval Operations; and Admiral Allen, commandant of the Coast Guard) endorses strengthening a traditionally powerful Navy/Marine relationship.

As the Marine Corps looks to clarify its functions and roles in the future, it is evident General Conway is uneasy with the impact Iraq has on the Corps and its ability to conduct others' tasks associated with its mission. In a recent *Wall Street Journal* interview.[1] General Conway discussed two related concerns about the war: that in order to fight this war, the Marine Corps could be transformed into just another "land army"; and, if that should happen, that it would lose the flexibility and expeditionary culture that has made it a powerful military force. The Corps was built originally to live aboard ships and wade ashore to confront emerging threats far from home. It has long prided itself in being "first to the fight" relying on speed, agility, and tenacity to win battles. It's a small, offensive outfit that has its own attack aircraft, but not its own medics, preferring to rely on Navy corpsmen to care for its wounded.

The Marine Corps must continue to meet its mission in Iraq and most recently its requirement to provide a Marine Expeditionary Unit and an infantry battalion to Afghanistan, but it must also look forward to ensure we are building the forces and procuring the equipment that will continue to make the Corps one of the world's best fighting organizations. In order to accomplish that task, the Corps must look to expand its capacity by building new capability sets for engagement and security cooperation activities. **The Marines' core service competency must remain its ability to perform forcible entry.**

As the Marine Corps continues to fulfill its requirements in Iraq as well as provide an additional 3,200 Marines to help improve warfare capabilities in Afghanistan, it must continue to be forward-leaning in its thinking as it attempts to grow the force by 27,000 personnel. As the Corps looks forward to the upcoming QDR, it has a couple of important elements of that growth that will need to be addressed: the attendant MILCON (barracks and training capacity) and commensurate equipment to ensure the Marine Corps will be ready when the Nation calls. As part of his House Armed Services Committee testimony in December 2007, the commandant expressed the value of amphibious ships is too often assessed exclusively in terms of forcible entry. This discounts their usefulness across the range of operations and the necessity for Marines embarked aboard amphibious ships to meet Phase 0 demands. The Marine Air-Ground Task Force (MAGTF) and the flexibility and adaptability it brings to the battlefield are unique to our Armed Services. To help the Marine Corps maintain this tremendous capability, the commandant has made it a priority to replace legacy aircraft with newer equipment such as the Joint Strike Fighter, MV-22, H-1 upgrades, and CH-53K. This will ensure that the Corps maintains its war fighting advantage for our Nation in the years to come.[2]

Finally, with the release of its "Long War Concept" the Marine Corps has argued that it must never lose its capability to defeat conventional foes. However, because of the continued challenges of the 21st Century, it must be able to participate in the "building of partner nation capacity." In this vain, the Corps could find itself involved in humanitarian assistance, disaster relief or perhaps in security cooperation with other governmental agencies or America's allies.

US Air Force. The US Air Force, alongside the US Navy, is regarded as strategic deterrent force that controls the skies over the battlefield. It prides itself as being the best air, space, and cyberservice in the world. Without fail, since 1953, it has ensured the safety of US ground forces by deterring and defeating enemy airpower and significantly enhancing ground forces' military operational effectiveness. The Air Force also provides two of the nation's three primary strategic deterrence tools: ICBMs and long-range bombers. Airmen can hold any target in the world at risk.

The Air Force faces pressure to both reduce legacy platform costs and associated risk caused by an aging aircraft fleet while it modernizes. The need to modernize is driven by both unsustainable maintenance costs and rivals who continue to improve their capabilities. An example of unsustainable maintenance costs would be those associated with an aging aerial tanker fleet, first procured in the late 1950s. The Air Force ranks its modernization priorities in order as (1) the next generation tanker (KC-45A); (2) combat search and rescue aircraft replacement (CSAR-X); (3) recapitalization of aging space platforms (early warning and communications satellites); (4) Joint Strike Fighter (F-35 Lightning); and (5) (as directed by the 2006 QDR), a next generation long-range strike aircraft (bomber).[3]

Air Force readiness is driven largely by the age of its hardware. Older aircraft and support equipment require more maintenance and associated personnel to keep the fleet healthy. Thus, at some point, it becomes necessary to replace older aircraft before the fleet becomes prohibitively expensive to maintain. The need to continue investing in modernized platforms is buttressed by a list of threats that challenge future US air, space, and cyberoperations. These include development and export of double digit surface to air missiles, such as the SA-10/12; advanced fourth generation aircraft development, such as the SU-27/30; advanced weapons, such as the AA-12 AAM, "Black Shaheen" low observable cruise missile; new sensors, such as infra-red search and track on the SU-27 Russian fighter; and also, an increase in the number of adversaries who possess advanced air defenses, proliferated by Russia and China since US airpower superiority demonstrated in Desert Storm, Allied Force, Operation Enduring Freedom, and Operation Iraqi Freedom.[4]

The Air Force is committed to force modernization, believing that not doing so will result in loss of competitive advantage against potential competitors. The service is also pressured by the threat of closing production lines and the inability or long lead times required of the US industrial base to recover from such a setback. The next QDR could challenge all of the services, including the Air Force, to do a better job of bundling capabilities that avoid redundancy. For the Air Force, this means re-looking at the executive agent status of airlift, cyber-operations, and tactical airpower, to name a few. **The service will advance its QDR and roles and functions arguments based upon the central belief that it is paramount to keep our ground forces safe from enemy air forces, that is, to maintain air, space, and cybersuperiority.**

Aside from its top five programmatic priorities presented previously, the Air Force is likely to concern itself with force sizing metrics (currently set at 330,000 personnel), limits on use of reserve component forces, COIN [counterinsurgency] doctrine, international cooperation, interagency reform, and re-casting itself as the premiere future thinker.[5] First, the Air Force needs something beyond 1-4-2-1 and capabilities-based planning to argue its future force structure. Strong possibilities include the war games and red teaming concepts espoused in the discussion on a persistent QDR. A new force planning construct lends objective, measurable credibility to proposed future force structures. The Air Force, like other services, is concerned about dependence and over-reliance upon Reserve component forces to execute its mission. This is because the Reserve component has shifted from a traditionally strategic reserve to an operational reserve, used routinely. Among the problems associated with this shift is the realization that Reserve forces are not closely enough aligned with the mission sets currently in demand. Thus, there is a need to re-evaluate Reserve roles and functions as well as the limits of mobilization.

Some of the best candidates for the Air Force QDR focus will likely arise from a response to the Army's Counter-insurgency manual FM 3-24 and its desire to re-instill credibility within its nuclear deterrence mission. Critics cite FM 3-24 as dismissing airpower as an Army support function, primarily providing air-lift and surveillance for ground forces. To bolster COIN doc-trine, the Air Force should be quick to point out that airpower brings speeds, mass, and precision to ground forces encumbered by terrain and distance, and does so with minimal collateral damage. As a primary US strategic deterrent force, the service should use the QDR to rebuild and refocus its nuclear bomber and ICBM [intercontinental ballistic missile] capabilities. COIN capabilities will bolster the services need for more unmanned ISR [intelligence, surveillance, and reconaissance], tankers, and airlift (to support a growing Army and Marine Corps), as it defends its ability to weaken and defeat other future adversaries with minimal ground force employment.[6]

The Air Force is likely to focus on its future relationship with the US interagency as well as key allies. Many Air Force operations work with or rely upon allies and interagency partners. Thus one can expect the Air Force to fully support growing co-operation with allies through exercises and "building partnership capacity" (which includes foreign internal defense, arm sales, training, education, humanitarian assistance, disaster relief, etc.). The service will also likely be a strong backer of efforts to reform the interagency by strengthening its deployable capabilities and operational planning functions.

Notes

1. Miniter, "First to the Fight."
2. Gen James T. Conway, commandant of the Marine Corps, statement before the House Armed Services Committee on Marine Corps.
3. Maj Gen Paul Selva, AF/A8X, briefing to Air Force Fellows, 31 July 2007.
4. Ibid.
5. Michéle Flournoy, remarks to the Air Staff, 20 April 2005.
6. John Tirpak, "The New Counterinsurgency."

Bibliography

Benton, Morgan C. CIS (Computer Information System) 350–Computers, Society, and Ethics. http://www.globalissues.org/Geopolitics/ArmsTrade/Spending.asp#WorldMilitarySpending.

Blaker, James. "The QDR: An Assessment." *Progressive Policy Institute Backgrounder*, 20 May 1997.

Brimley, Shawn, Bacevich Fellow. The Center for a New American Security, December 2007.

Brower, Michael D. "QDR for Dummies," 16 May 1997. http://www4.army.mil/ocpa/read.php?story_id_key=281799.

Congressional Budget Office. "The Long-Term Implications of Current Defense Plans: Detailed Update for Fiscal Year 2007."

Conway, Gen James T., commandant of the Marine Corps. Statement before the House Armed Services Committee on the Marine Corps, 1 March 2007. http://www.globalsecurity.org/military/library/congress/2007_hr/070301-skelton_openingnavyposture.htm.

Correll, John T. "In Pursuit of Strategy." *Air Force Magazine* 84, no. 8: (August 2001). http://www.afa.org/magazine/Aug2001/0801watch.asp.

Crawley, Vince. "No Crystal Ball for Threats to the Homeland." *Federal Times*, 17 December 2005.

Department of Defense (DOD). "Chairman's Assessment of the 2006 Quadrennial Defense Review." Introduction, A-3. http://www.comw.org/qdr/qdr2006.pdf.

———. "Directive (DODD) 5100.1," 1 August 2002.

———. "The Quadrennial Defense Review 1997," May 1997.

———. "The Quadrennial Defense Review 2001," September 2001.

———. "The Quadrennial Defense Review 2006," February 2006.

DOD News Briefing. "The Quadrennial Defense Review," 19 May 1997.

Donnelly, Tom. "Kill the QDR." *Armed Forces Journal*, February 2006. http://www.armedforcesjournal.com.

England, Gordon, deputy secretary of defense. Remarks at event organized by the Center for Strategic and International Studies (CSIS). St. Regis Hotel, Washington, DC, 1 February 2006.

Flournoy, Michèle A. "Did the Pentagon Get the Quadrennial Defense Review Right?" *Washington Quarterly* 29, no. 2 (Spring 2006): 67–84. http://www.comw.org/qdr/fulltext/ 0603flournoy.pdf.

———. Remarks. "Goldwater-Nichols: A Critical Look." CSIS, 24 January 2008.

———. Transcript on Remarks to the Air Staff, 20 April 2005.

Government Accounting Office. "John Warner National Defense Authorization Act for Fiscal Year 2007," Pub. Law No. 109–364, §1031 (2006); GAO-07-709.

———. "Quadrennial Defense Review: Future Reviews Could Benefit from Improved Department of Defense Analyses and Changes to Legislative Requirements." *Study 07-709*, September 2006, 10–13.

Grossman, Elaine M. "Key Review Offers Scant Guidance on Handling '4th Generation' Threats." *Inside the Pentagon*, 4 October 2001, 1.

Gunzinger, Mark. "Beyond the Bottom-Up Review." National War College, 1996. http://www.ndu.edu/inss/books/Books%20 -%202000/essa/essabtbu.html.

Henry, Ryan. "Defense Transformation and the 2005 Quadrennial Defense Review." *Parameters* 35, no. 4 (Winter 2005–06): 8.

Jaffe, Lorna. "The Development of the Base Force 1989–1992." Washington, DC: Pentagon, Joint History Office, 1993, 12.

Kaplan, Fred. "Rumsfeld Surrenders: The QDR Dashes His Dreams of Military Transformation." *Slate*, 3 February 2006. http://rempost.blogspot.com/2006/02/rumsfeld -surrenders-qdr-dashes-his.html.

Krepinevich, Andrew. "The Quadrennial Defense Review: Transforming to Meet Tomorrow's Security Challenges." Center for Strategic and Budgetary Assessments, 17 March 2006, 7–9.

Kuehl, Daniel T., and Charles E. Miller. "Roles, Missions, and Functions: Terms of Debate." *Joint Forces Quarterly*, Summer 2004. http://www.ndu.edu/inss/Press/jfq_pages/ debate5.pdf.

McKenzie, Kenneth F., Jr. "Assessing Risk: Enabling Sound Defense Decisions." In *QDR 2001: Strategy-Driven Choices for America's Security*. Washington, DC: National Defense University Press, 2001. http://www.ndu.edu/inss/press/qdr_2001/sdcasch07.html.

Miniter, Brendan. "First to the Fight." *Wall Street Journal*, 12 January 2008. http://online.wsj.com/article/SB120010.425941885571.html?mod=opinion_main_commentaries

Murdock, Clark. "An Assessment of the 2006 QDR." http://www.csis.org/component/option,com_csis_progj.

———. Correspondence with Michèle Flournoy, 29 December 2005. In Michèle A. Flournoy, "Did the Pentagon Get the Quadrennial Defense Review Right?" *Washington Quarterly* 29, no. 2 (Spring 2006): 67–84. http://www.comw.org/qdr/fulltext/0603flournoy.pdf.

Murdock, Clark A., Michèle A. Flournoy, Kurt M. Campbell, Pierre A. Chao, Julianne Smith, Anne A. Witkowsky, and Christine E. Wormuth. "Beyond Goldwater Nichols: Defense Reform for a New Strategic Era—Phase II Report." Washington, DC: CSIS Press, 2005.

National Defense Authorization Act of 1996. Public Law 104-201, Subtitle B, "Force Structure Review." Sections 921–26.

Osowski, Christine. "Approaching the QDR as a Process." *Avascent Review* no.10, March 2006, 20–21.

Patterson, Dean, and Lenny Richoux. "Put the '08 QDR to Use." *Defense News*, 19 November 2007, 37.

Ratman, Gopal. "QDR May Devolve into a Budget-Cutting Recipe." *Defense News*, 7 November 2005, 37.

Rumsfeld, Donald H., secretary of defense. Pentagon Press Conference, 1 February 2006.

SAF/FMBP (Air Force Budget Programs). "Introduction to PPBE," April 2008. Lt Col Charles Shea (e-mail).

Selva, Maj Gen Paul, AF/A8X. Briefing to Air Force Fellows, 31 July 2007.

Sinclair, Upton, ed. "The Cry for Justice: An Anthology of the Literature of Social Protest." New York, NY: Barricade Books, 1915.

Tangredi, Sam J. "All Possible Wars? Towards a Consensus View of the Future Security Environment: 2001–2025."

McNair Paper 63, chap. 4, "Assumptions on National Strategy," November 2000.

Tiron, Roxana. "Pentagon Strategists Ponder Value of High-Tech Weapons." *National Defense Magazine*, March 2005. http://www.diig-csis.org/news/article.asp?ARTICLE_ID=33&.

Tirpak, John. "The New Counterinsurgency; Airpower to the Rear; That Satellite is Toast. . . " *Air Force Magazine* 90, no. 3 (March 2007). http://www.globalissues.org/Geopolitics/ArmsTrade/Spending.asp.

US House, Committee on Armed Services. "CDR: Fact Sheet." Washington, DC. http://www.house.gov/hasc/CDR/CDRFactSheet.pdf.

———. H.R. 3198: "Quadrennial National Security Review Act." http://www.govtrack.us.

Rethinking the QDR

The Case for a Persistent Defense Review

Air University Press Team

Editor
Dr. Richard Bailey

Copy Editor
Andrew Thayer

Cover Art and Book Design
Steven C. Garst

Illustrations
Susan Fair

*Composition and
Prepress Production*
Vivian O'Neal

Quality Review
Mary J. Moore

Print Preparation
Diane Clark

Distribution
Diane Clark

www.ingramcontent.com/pod-product-compliance
Lightning Source LLC
Chambersburg PA
CBHW082147290526
45794CB00008B/3189